VOICES OF THE GREAT DEPRESSION—THE 1930'S

By Cinda Anderson

ISBN: 0-75966-878-7

This book is printed on acid free paper.

1stBooks - rev. 12/11/01

INTRODUCTION

These are just a few voices who were willing to tell bits and pieces of their individual and family stories about a period of our history known as The Great Depression. From 1929 through 1939, banks failed, the stock market crashed, and resulted in putting hundreds and thousands of people drifted over the United States trying to find work and to survive for yet another day.

The population of the United States in 1930 was 123,202,624. By 1931, the number of people reported out of work was 9,000,000. There were 2,294 banks that failed during the year of 1931. Private charity was unable to cope with the situation of the needy. Companies cut wages of their workers.

Industrial production dropped 12 percent during the year 1933. Many people found themselves working for as little as 10 cents an hour. During this year, the estimate was that one third of the labor force was out of work.

In 1934, some of the unemployed found jobs. Farm prices increased because of subsidies and crop limitations. A drought seized the country.

In 1935, the Social Security Act passed. Our President at this time is President Roosevelt. A work relief program was strengthening the economy.

The economy brightened in 1936. There was fear by some that social legislation would erode freedom, liberty and individualism.

Roosevelt continued with his plans of social welfare. The unemployed still numbered 7,000,000. Industrial production and agricultural output rose. 1936 was the first year the word "recession" was used.

1938 revealed the stock market reaching its lowest point in four years. The recession continued to worsen.

In 1939, Germany moved into Czechoslovakia. England and France declare war on Germany. President Roosevelt appealed for legislation to bolster our nation's defenses as Americans watched in dismay the events in Europe.

As a child, I heard stories of the Great Depression. I listened intently to my parents and my grandparents talking of bad and sad times. I never got bored with their stories over the years, and invariably when new people of the older generation came into my life, my first question was always, "What were things like for you during the Great Depression?"

My fascination continues to this day and below are personal tales from people around the country whose voices are slowly being silenced with death and infirmity. This story is their story. Their expressions, grammar, and explanations are recorded as they were received or told.

THE SOUTH

"Webster's dictionary describes a Depression as: 'a dent, a hollow, a deep indentation, an impression.' That it was, that it was - the Great Depression, I mean.

It made a deep hole in our way of life, in our values, in our attitudes, in our finances, and in every phase of our living. It made a deep and lasting impression. One that changed our lives forever.

If anyone was a child of "The Depression" and survived, I was.

Disaster struck and often overnight. Banks closed with no warning. Businesses were lost. Farms were lost. Homes were lost. Jobs were lost. There was no money except a small amount that people just happened to have at home and there was no where to get any more.

My family lost two businesses, our farm, and our home. We were able to live in the house for a while.

My father got a job as head of the W.P.A. I remember fathers of my friends coming to our house at night begging for work, digging ditches even. These were professional people and business leaders along with blue-collar workers.

During the winter of 1931-32 not one young person in my home town of Mullins was able to go to college.

Our times were not all bad. We made our own fun. Many of the boys had gone to join the CCC. They lived in camps patterned after army camps and performed community work. They were involved in many worthwhile permanent projects.

Those of us who were at home kept ourselves busy. There were no movies, no money, no 'dragging Main Street' in a car, and no gas. We walked up and down the streets at night in groups singing, talking, and laughing about what we did when we were young! We sat on porches and on steps in warm weather, and we cooked candy or cake, or sometimes even made a full meal. When we cooked, each person brought an ingredient - sugar, milk, eggs, flour, etc. - depending on what was on our menu. I remember this was very good- both the food and the fellowship.

We were fortunate because we had a garden, a cow, and chickens. From these, we lived and we shared.

A former cook, whom we could no longer afford, was trying to raise a family of five small children. She too ate from our garden. She helped plant and worked it. Each morning, she came down to the house and got milk for her children. She was also allowed to cut down a big chinaberry tree to use for firewood.

During the Depression, there was no Wood yard fund, no welfare, no United Way, and no organized charities. There was no where to go for help except to friends who were all in the same boat.

We had pigeons, but I refused to allow my father to eat or give away the squabs! So, he would slip out at night and take them to friends. They were not considered a delicacy. They were a way of survival!

New clothes were not even thought about. We swapped or altered them to appear different.

During the summer, the boys worked in tobacco, either in the fields cropping and dragging or under the shed (barn) stringing and curing. To cure the tobacco, the wood-burning fire must be kept at a constant temperature for many, many hours. For this reason, it was necessary for someone to be there to tend it around the clock.

One of our most 'fun' times was having a chicken bog and a watermelon cuttin' at a tobacco barn. The boys would build a fire under a big, black, iron wash pot (which they took to the barn in a tobacco 'drag' pulled by a mule). In the pot filled with water was put a big, fat, cleaned hen and after the water had started boiling. The hen cooked as the tobacco cured. A watermelon or two or three was put in the nearby rivers or in another wash pot if there was no river close by and covered with ice.

Late in the afternoon, the girls would come down with iced tea, slaw, boiled eggs, and sometimes a cake or cookies. Earlier in the afternoon, after the chicken was done, the rice was put in the pot with the chicken and the broth and cooked.

By the time the girls arrived, the rice was done and the hard-boiled eggs were added. By now all the boys had come in from the fields, and we had a grand time. There was fun, fellowship, and wonderful food with friends. There is nothing better than this!

My father's health failed finally after much work and worry, and heartache. My mother went back to teaching and was paid with 'script'. Script was a paper agreement which stores cashed for a fee.

A friend once said years later, the Depression toughened us and tossed us about, but made us appreciate the real values of life. It made us very humble and aware of the needs of others. It made us appreciative of what we had even though it was much less than what we had had only a short time earlier!

The Great Depression. It was the worst of times. It was the best of times. It was a time of caring for each other and sharing with each other. It was a time of strengthening our faith, and deepening our beliefs. It was a time of learning that something that had been so important before was no longer important at all.

It was a time of vivid memories, bittersweet though they may be, which were etched on the heart and never forgotten. But, I would not want to go back and visit!"

- MRH - South Carolina

2

.   .   .

"I was just a kid during the Depression, and we lived on a farm out in the country. They only time I saw my mother cry was during this time. My parents had just built a house on the farm. You couldn't make a decent living on a farm even during those days, but Daddy decided to make a go at dairy farming because they were subsidized pretty heavily.

Our house was the only house in the area that had a water pump on the inside at that time. It was not an automatic water pump, but a pump where you pumped water by hand. Momma cried on that day because she did not know how they were going to make it.

We always had food at the house. Everything we ate was always served on a bed of rice. Momma would take a quart of tomatoes, a quart of okra, and a quart of green beans, and place them in a pot, and then, serve it over a bed of rice. We would get two meals out of this for a family of six.

My mother's worst meals were when she would stew potatoes, and then place them over a bed of rice. I always hated eating potatoes over rice. I thought it was a terrible meal.

I was going to school at the time, and each day the bus would drop us off at the local store. This store was the only place in the country where we could buy school supplies, or if we had the money, candy.

One day I got it in my head that I just had to have a new tablet for school. It cost a nickel. I went home and asked my mother for a nickel. She told me to ask Daddy out in the barn because she did not have any money.

I went to Daddy, and he reached deep into his pockets, rummaged through his change, and gave me my nickel. The next day I bought my tablet, and then I cried all day long at school because I really did not need that tablet in the first place. I felt bad that Mother and Daddy may have needed that nickel for other things.

My cousin, who is 14 years older than I am, taught me all the nicer and finer things in life. She lived in a small town and invited me to spend the summer with her.

While I was there, they had a bridal shower for someone. It was there I first became aware of how to properly do things with society. I remember we had an ice cream square with a sugar bell on top. I thought it was the grandest thing in the world.

I found out there was no Santa Claus one year when the whole family was sick with the flu. During those years, people stayed away from you when you had the flu. I recall hearing my uncle speaking to my father through the window. My father told him to do what he could for Christmas. That was the year we got a peppermint stick and an orange, and I found out there was no Santa Claus.

We had chickens on the farm for eggs. I hated going to get eggs because the hens would peck at you. Worst of all was every once in a while you would get a hen to move off its perch only to find a chicken snake would be coiled up inside the nest. I would start to scream then for my mother to come quick. I didn't want anything to do with snakes."
- South Carolina

.   .   .

"I was just a kid growing up wild in the mountains of West Virginia. I did not know that my torn pants were a sign of being poor. I also did not care whether I had shoes on my feet. I did not see a banana until I was 18 years old."
- West Virginia
..."We always had food to eat - even if it was only biscuits and syrup - we always had food."
-South Carolina

.   .   .

"We knew the stock market crashed. We were aware the banks had failed. We were so poor already it didn't make any difference."
- Georgia

.   .   .

"My most vivid memory of the depression was that we had no money. There were no vacations or good times.

My father lost his home and we relied on charity and gardens and part-time jobs to get food on the table. When family became ill, we prayed. We lived far from our family and moved in with relatives when the depression hit. We were thankful we were alive and my favorite holiday was Christmas. We were all aware of the depression and that other people were out of work and helped strangers on their way as they came to us.

I only had one outfit. My favorite meal was eggs, ham and beans, and my worst meal was cabbage soup.

We did a lot of reading and listened to the radio. I particularly liked Amos & Andy."
- Georgia

.   .   .

"It was a time when people lived very simple lives as compared to today. Since I was born just before the Great Depression of the late twenties, my earliest memories are of a life that was filled with long days of hard work and only the bare necessities of life.

One of my first memories was of something that still fascinates me until this day - bridges. Many of the smaller streams did not have bridges to cross over. Wagons and buggies with a team of mules or horses had to wade the stream and pull the vehicle across. The T-Model cars crossed the same way since that was the transition period from the wagon to the car.

The most fascinating of all to me was the Saluda River that flowed near my grandmother's home. There were few bridges before Lake Murray was built and people crossed larger streams by ferries. We would go visit my grandmother and walk with other family members to see the attendant pull the barge across the river by a rope that had been tied at both sides of the river.

He had a small one-room cabin to protect him from the rain and the cold of winter while he waited for someone to cross the river. I never knew if he was paid for this service. This way people could attend Macedonia Church and shop at Prosperity or Newberry and even visit family and friends.

Animals were also transported the same way still hitched to the vehicle. They were very docile while on the water. People would return the same way by calling out to the attendant to come for them. It was an awesome and interesting sight probably because I was a small child at that time."

- South Carolina

.   .   .

"We lived seven miles from Atlanta, Georgia during the time of the Great Depression. We were very aware of news in the Atlanta area and my most vivid memory is the large number of suicides in the area, many of which were by jumping from the tall buildings in Atlanta.

One of my saddest memories was when the father of one of my friends killed himself by gunshot. This friend later became a Methodist minister and chaplain in the U.S. Navy. He lost his life in one of the earlier naval engagements in the Pacific during World War II.

My happiest memory was that I was selected to have the most desired Atlanta Journal paper route in Decatur, Georgia. I made about $5.00 per week at this job and therefore could buy some wants that I otherwise could not have had during this time.

Gifts during this period of time was usually a new pair of trousers (knickers) or some other item of clothing. Fireworks were also a very welcome gift when the occasion called for it.

Money for the family came from selling produce from our garden. We lived on a large city lot (about 1 1/2 acres) and had many fig trees, raspberry vines, and a large truck garden. A pint of figs brought 15 cents, a quarter brought 25 cents. On a good day, we would pick and sell 40 quarts of figs.

Our home was right beside the street car track that ran into Atlanta. One of the stops was in front of our house and many people who still had a job would buy some of the produce when they got off the street car at our stop.

My father was out of work for about three years. I was very conscious of the scarcity of work for him and others.

My mother never turned away anyone who came to the door asking for something to eat. It seems that she always had some cornbread and vegetable soup on hand. She would share with those who were in need, especially black people. I remember one, (old Aunt Martha was what we called her), who was a daily caller at our door and who was never turned away.

When I was in college, my father would sometimes send me a dollar bill when he could afford it. I thought I was rich. I was able to buy a coke, an egg sandwich, and still had money leftover. (We did not leave tips for food services.)

My favorite meal was melted cheese on a platter of soda crackers. After I became "sophisticated," I learned that the dish was Welsh Rarebit!

My clothes consisted of several pairs of overalls and one Sunday outfit. When it came to faith, my family had always been one of great faith and they never lost it. I learned from them to deal with whatever life "handed" one."

- Georgia

.   .   .

"I have never seen worse times than those during the Great Depression. The Nation was in terrible financial shape. People were broke, and there was no money and no jobs. At the time, I was working for Edgefield County and things were so bad, all county officials voluntarily reduced their salaries. I was told that since I made so little I did not have to take a pay cut, but I did anyhow. Suffice it to say, I hope the United States never goes through another period of economic distress like the Depression ever again."

- South Carolina

.   .   .

"When my grandfather returned from the Great War, he ventured to Wilmington, North Carolina and found a job as a cashier for the city's Water Department. This began an almost lifelong career in service to the city. He was soon recognized as an aspiring, capable, young man and was promoted to tax collector, and a year later to city clerk and treasurer.

My grandfather was just as stunned by the crash of the stock market in 1929 as the rest of the nation. There were no statistics to predict the collapse. All banks were closed with no way of attaining funds for anything.

The city clerk/treasurer was responsible to distribute the payroll for city employees in cash as was customary. This cash, however, was not available.

As a result, the city began issuing script (a kind of receipt to be cashed later when funds were freed).

At first, Wilmington businesses were reluctant to accept this as currency but soon acknowledged it to increase their sharply declined sales. Soon, the city would receive the script back where it had originated in the form of taxes. The use of script went on for three months, and all the script was repaid in six months after its use began.

Although many in the town lost their jobs, my grandfather was fortunate to keep his. Even though the economy came to a stop, city services such as trash collecting still had to be rendered and city employees continued their work even without assurance of pay.

During the first week, it was difficult to buy food. However, there were backyard gardens to depend on. With no cash to buy things, citizens grew hungry and grocery stores closed while food rotted on their shelves. Soon, some grocers reopened in order to serve the people who could pay. For those who could not, bread lines, often a half a mile long, were available. No one could pay anyone else without cash, and banks would not even cash their own checks. Under Hoover, the economy went from bad to worse resulting in the election of Franklin D. Roosevelt in 1932.

The new president took immediate action to combat the economic problems. Recovery programs of the New Deal began to reach the city as FDR's National Recovery Administration passed through Congress. Part of this administration included the Public Works Administration which grandfather felt was the most helpful law passed in the New Deal.

Public Works projects were completed by the unemployed for five dollars per five-day week and were funded sixty percent by the federal and forty percent by the local governments. Citizens volunteered to administer the P.W.A.

Many new projects began in Wilmington. For example, a road around Greenfield Lake was built to add a scenic drive to the city. Later, the Public Works Administration helped fund the rebuilding of city hall. It also helped with the building of many other parks and roads as well.

With all of FDR's efforts, the economic recovery was still very slow with a substantial slump in 1937. Although no statistics were available to show actual growth or decline, grandfather felt the war speeded up the ending of the Depression."

- North Carolina

•   •   •

"I was born in Kansas but moved with my family to Florida in 1925. This was during a time that was called "The Florida Boom." I think my father had visions of getting rich there.

My memories of that time are rather vague, but I recall hearing about the "Big Crash" and the closing of banks in 1928. It did not really affect us except as the Depression began to spread.

My father was in the jewelry business, and it was not long before he began to feel the effects of the Depression.

The only thing I remember about that early time was that we had to move from a home my parents had bought, and from that time on, we lived in smaller, rented houses.

However, this did not bother me because we moved nearer my school friends. I remember a very happy childhood.

My mother made most of my clothes, and I always had plenty of clothes and food. I can remember my mother feeding tramps or hoboes who came to our door asking for work or food. I do not think she ever refused them.

I never felt deprived of anything. I believe this was because nearly everyone I knew was in more or less the same financial situation.

My most vivid and saddest memory of those times was near the end of the depression. When I graduated from high school, I wanted desperately to go on to college. My parents managed to send me where I wanted to go for one year. After the year was over, they told me they could not afford for me to go back. However, I was able to get a job and saved enough to go back after two years."

DM - Florida

.   .   .

"I graduated from high school in 1928. The week after graduation, I started college at East Tennessee State Teachers College (now known as East Tennessee State University). The only vacation I had for the next five years was one week at Christmas.

After five quarters at college, I was hired by the Unicoi County System to teach primer, first, second, and third grades. I also taught sixth, seventh and eighth grade English after recess in the afternoons. The school was in Rocky Fork, Tennessee. It was started as a Presbyterian Mission School and I lived in their home. It was located near Flag Pond in the mountains between Erwin, Tennessee and Asheville, North Carolina.

I continued teaching and going to school until 1933 when I received by B.S. Degree. I was out of school on Friday and I started teaching on Monday.

The Depression really hit the school system in Tennessee in 1931. The last two years I spent at Rocky Fork I was paid by the county and the state in small amounts. They could not pay the full amount of back wages until 1933.

After graduation, I taught one year in Johnson City, my home town. I had 45 children in the morning, and after lunch, I taught 45 other children in the second grade.

My salary was $80, but I only received $20 in cash and $60 was in "Due Bills." The Due Bills could be accepted at face value for city taxes and at some department stores. The $20 in cash was used to pay for paper to duplicate schoolwork for the 90 children. There were work books published for this purposes, but no one could afford them.

The next year, I was hired by the Kingsport School system. We were paid in cash! I had a $10 raise! This time I had 48 children all day long. There were seven girls and forty-one boys.

During my next year (1935-36), the class was evenly split between boys and girls and I had about 30 children. I taught at the schools until 1940 when I was married. The children in the three schools where I taught were cooperative and fun to teach.

Kingsport, Tennessee was a small town, but several industries started here. It was one of the few school systems that paid cash during the Depression. The teachers came from Florida, Georgia, Iowa, Missouri, Nebraska, Kentucky and many other states."

\- ECS - Tennessee

.   .   .

"I was born in Chester, South Carolina and lived in the same house until I went away to Erskine College in 1935. The family's modest sized house was painted white originally, but later was repainted a cream color. The house was kept in the family until 1973.

We were a family of six boys and there was hardly room for anyone else to live with us. The house was originally one and one-half stories, but as the family grew, it became necessary to "Raise the roof." The house was on a narrow lot (75 feet wide) at the corner of College and Hinton Streets. College Street terminated at Hinton.

Mr. grandparents, Judge and Mrs. J. K. Henry, lived in a large house on Hinton Street which faced down the length of College Street. The Henrys had a large family of three sons and four daughters who all lived until adulthood. At one time, most of the children lived within two blocks of my grandparents house. Because family was all close by, it was not surprising on holidays, we all enjoyed a huge family dinner at their home.

Thanksgiving and Christmas was huge in terms of attendance. There were 20 to 30 of us and it was also huge in terms of food. Typically, we had roast turkey, rice and gravy, cornbread dressing, sweet potato pudding, macaroni and cheese, escalloped oysters, and beans. There were probably other vegetables of which I was not particularly fond and therefore do not remember.

The dessert was nearly always fruit cake and ambrosia which was made from fresh orange section and freshly grated coconut. Salted, roasted pecans were also served.

The adults ate at one large and two smaller tables in the huge dining room while the children ate at table on the back sun porch. You knew you had "Arrived" in the family when you graduated from the sun porch to the dining room.

In the early 1930's, despite the severe economic depression being experienced, it became mandatory to enlarge our house because of the growth of the family. The lower level consisted of a living room, a side hall, one bedroom, a bath, a dining room, a kitchen, a back porch and several closets. The upper level contained one modest sized bedroom, a storage or "Plunder" room and several closets. In remodeling, the roof was actually raised so that the upper floor became a full floor instead of a half upper story. After the change, there were one large and two smaller bedrooms and a bath as well as several closets on the second floor. Passage from the front to the rear of the house could be made either from the hall through the dining room or from the bedroom through the bath.

Our custom for our house was for Santa Claus to visit the dining room. This room had a fireplace. It was the family rule on Christmas morning to have the dining room doors locked. We had to have our breakfast in the kitchen before we were allowed to see what Santa had brought us.

Our house was originally heated by fireplaces in most of the rooms. Later, Dad installed a coal burning furnace which was located in the center of the house. It heated this area more than generously, but the extremities of the house tended to remain cold. Still later, he had the house insulated by blowing insulation into the side walls. Cold air return ducts were also installed from the perimeter of the house back to the furnace. This made the house much more comfortable, but we still used the fireplace in the living room because of the extra heat it provided.

Coal was most often burned in the fireplace. We had a blower for this fireplace which was a fitted metal plate that could be placed over the upper part of the grate and it greatly increased the draft. The grate was quickly brought to a red hot condition and it would heat the room in a hurry.

My father was something of a inventor. An invention I took for granted was a merry-go-round. This was situated in our side yard just outside of the dining room. The base was a 12" x 12" concrete block which had centered vertically a steel rod which was made from an automobile axle. Atop this was a seven-foot cedar pole about 7" in diameter. The bottom of the pole had a central hole just large enough to slip down over the old axle. At the top of the pole was a double pulley (also a recycled part of a car). The top part of the double pulley was sturdily positioned by cables running to the corner of the house and several trees. About a foot below the top, Dad had drilled three horizontal holes to take three 1 1/2" steel pipes which were eight feet long and evenly spaced around the central pole radially. The end of each pie was guyed back to the lower pulley. From the end of each pipe, a swing was hung. Some were simple boards and others were seats with a safety bar in front for the smaller children. A horizontal iron bar inserted in the cedar pole at waste level and was used to turn the device. It was a marvelous contraption and we were the envy of the neighborhood.

Another invention of my father was secret locks on the doors to the basement and to a number of backyard sheds. Our backyard opened on Hinton Street and this street was fairly heavy with traffic. It was easy for a passersby to get into the backyard. To protect things, Dad invented ingenious hidden locks to the door opening on the yard. There would be a series of cords leading to a pull wire several feet from the door itself. By pulling this unobtrusive wire ring, the latch was lifted and the door could be opened. It was unlikely an intruder noticed the pull wire and dad had release devices like this on six or more entry doors.

Soon after the house was remodeled, I had a harrowing experience. It was Christmas and time for fireworks to be used. Clarke, my brother, sent me upstairs to the room we shared to get some Big Chiefs (4" firecrackers) from his drawers. While I was getting these, I noticed a pistol he had borrowed from a friend to take on a hunting trip.

I could not resist the temptation and pulled the pistol out and aimed it about the room. I casually pulled the trigger because I thought it was unloaded. There was a big explosion and I almost fainted.

I frantically began to search the room to find where the bullet had struck. After a while, I found it lodged in a door across the hall. I dug out the ball and quickly filled the hole with some putty from the garage. Because of the noise of firecrackers exploding in the neighborhood, no one had noticed the shot and I made sure I did not mention it.

Months later, Mother discovered the patch and was very upset about the damage to the newly refinished upstairs. During dinner, she began to go around the table and asked each son if they knew the cause of the blemish. I sat back squirming in panic. Just as she reached me, the phone rang. When she got back from the call, she forgot where she was in the line-up and skipped over me to one of my other brothers. You can be sure I volunteered no information. (Many year later, I told her the details of the matter, and by that time, it was cause for much amusement)

Radio was in its infancy when I was growing up. Our first radio was a single tube, battery operated model. You had to listened to it through earphones. There was often a big squabble over who of the eight persons in the house got to listen. Sometimes we would dismount the earphones from the headset and place them in a large metal waste basket. They would faintly act like a loud speaker.

Later, we got a five tube set with a separate loudspeaker which was an accessory. Some of the programs that caught our fancy were Amos and Andy, Ben Bernie, and big bands like Glenn Miller, Tommy Dorsey, Glenn Gray and

Erskine Hawkins. My parents were quite interested in baseball and always listened to the World Series on the radio.

Chester was a small town of about 6,000 people when I was a child. The main industry was three cotton mills where baled cotton was woven into cotton fabric. The labor moved became active in the South in the early 1930's and there were many attempts to organize the local cotton mills. Oddly enough, most of the workers were against the union, and you can be sure management opposed them. During one period of agitation, the National Guard was called up and set up machine gun emplacements around the mills. This action was considered entirely proper in the South at that time.

One of our favorite games we played was "Kick the Can." I believe this game came from "Kick the Wicket," but we did not know what a wicket was and we had plenty of cans. A large can was placed in a circle in the front yard. One of the strongest kids got a running start and kicked it as far as he could. Everyone, except the person who was "It", immediately ran and hid somewhere while "It" had to retrieve the can and return it to the circle before he could start looking for the others. If he spotted someone and touched the can before the spotted person did, then that person became a "Prisoner" and had to sit on the front steps. If one of the "Hiders" slipped back to the front and kicked the can again, all the prisoners were free and could go hide again. With a large group, our games would last for many hours or until we got tired of it.

We also used to have rubber gun battles. Money was scarce so we had to invent and make many of our toys. We would fashion crude rifles out of scrap wood and mount a clothes pin for a trigger. We cut rubber bands from sections of auto tire tubes and these were stretched from the "muzzle" back to be caught in the clothes pin. When the pin was depressed, the band was released and would fly for ten to fifteen feet. If you were hit by the flying rubber band, you were "Dead" for that game. The rubber bands did not sting unless they were fired from very close range. We even developed mutilple-shot rifles and long-barrel pistols. One time, I even tried to develop a rubber machine gun, but it never worked very well.

At times, we had a garden in the backyard. My parents were fond of vegetables, but they were not usually the favorites of the kids. We showed little enthusiasm for gardening except for tomatoes which everyone enjoyed.

Weeding was a particularly onerous task. One particularly obnoxious pest was called "nut grass." This plant had a small bulb set about 3 to 4 inches in the ground and was very hard to pull up. Someone advised us they only way to get rid of nut grass was to pull it up and pour kerosene down the hole. We never tried that.

In addition to the garden, we had a pear tree and several apple trees. Dad also had a grape vine he trained to grow on wires crisscrossed above the backyard. We only got a few grasp, but the vines provided a very desirable shady area in the backyard.

Dad was very interested in chickens. At one time, he had a flock of Plymouth Barred Rocks. These were housed in two large chicken houses at the edge of the back yard. Later, he tired of the chickens and converted the chicken houses to workshops. Because the street behind us was traveled heavily, there were problems with petty thievery from the storage and work shops. So, Dad invented various ingenious locks for the doors. There would appear to be no outside latch, but there was one on the inside, and by pulling a string or wire at a obscure, remote spot, the latch would open. Dad was so proud of his inventions that he demonstrated them often, and I believe this negated their usefulness.

We also kept a milk cow to provide milk for the large family. Dad was fond of Guernseys which tend to give milk with a fairly high butterfat content. In those days, no one worried about high animal fat, and the milk provided more butter. We had one cow that gave five gallons per day, which is a very high producer.

Once during the 1930's, our cow unexpectedly got sick and died. At the moment, Dad was particularly strapped for funds. So, Clarke and I offered to provide funds for another cow from our bank accounts. We paid $35 for her. With the acquisition of the cow, we also "Earned" the right to do the milking!

Milking must be done twice each day every day without exception or else the cow will go dry. Milking was not that hard, but it sure was regular. Usually we would take turns by the week to do the chore. Eventually, Dad repaid us for the cow, but we continued to do the milking as long as we had a cow.

When most people milk, they tend to use a three-legged stool and place the bucket on the ground. Not infrequently, the cow would move around during milking and sometimes knock over the bucket or stool or both.

To overcome this problem, Dad invented a milking seat. It was a sturdy bench about 40 inches long and with four strong legs. At one end, a round hole was cut into which the milking pail could be securely nested. The end of the seat containing the pail was slipped under the cow and the weight of the milker on the other end held it firmly on the ground. I never was aware of the cow knocking over this device.

The cow also was in the habit of swishing her tail to drive off flies. Being swatted in the face by a cow's tail was no fun, so I would separate the long terminal hair into two strands and loosely tie this around her leg. The result was no more swats in the face!"

- RWM - South Carolina

.　　　.　　　.

"During the Depression, we lived on a farm just outside of Lexington, South Carolina. We grew everything we needed. Our family has had this farm land since we received a land grant from Charles II of England.

We had our own chickens, cows and pigs for meat and our gardens. My father was a produce farmer and took his crops to the Farmer's Market in Columbia to sell. He sold tomatoes and squash in the summer, and in the winter, he sold turnips, spinach, and collards.

When daddy went to Columbia, it was a long trip and sometimes we would not see him for several days. There was a lot of stealing and robbing during the Depression. My father would take the money he got at the Farmer's Market and stuff it into his shoes. That way if someone tried to rob him they would not find any money on him.

When he returned from his trips, he would always bring us a bag of candies. My favorite was coconut dipped in different flavored frostings. There was chocolate, vanilla and lemon. He also brought us a wonderful watermelon candy, too.

We did not buy a lot in the Depression. In the winter, our family would butcher pigs for meat. Every part of the pig was used. We got liver puddings and sausage and lard and crackling from our pigs. There were times when we got tired of ham and bacon all the time. Then, daddy would sell a ham and get bologna, wieners and salmon for us. We felt that was an extra special treat.

Our family also belonged to a beef club. There were 16 members and every few weeks one of the member would butcher a cow. A log book was kept as to what each family received so that eventually all the parts of the cow, including the extra special good parts, were distributed to each family.

We had a well off the back porch. The water from this well was wonderfully cool at any time of the year. We hung our meats on ropes and put them in the well in order to keep it from spoiling.

Birthdays were basically just another day. However, my mother would make a cake for a celebration. In the summertime, we attended fund raisers that were held in the form of a picnic.

My mother cooked three meals a day. For breakfast, we had grits, eggs, ham, milk, and fresh fried chicken. There is nothing better than fried chicken in the morning. She also made delicious biscuits, and we would cover them up in lots syrup and butter.

We had farm workers helping daddy out. These were usually Nigras who lived on the outskirts of the farm. He used them as laborers and mother would fix them a meal.

There were times when hoboes came by. We were afraid of the hoboes, but mother fed anybody that came by. There were many times I remember two to three tables of people for lunch and we usually had chicken and pork.

At Christmas time, I only remember my sister and me receiving two dolls and maybe there were paper dolls as well. Mother saved coupons in order to get them for us. We did not receive a lot of toys.

For entertainment, we played lots of ball. My grandfather made balls for us out of pieces of inner tube tire. He would make the center of the balls out of this and then wrap, unraveled yarn from socks around and around it and then sew it up. Our bats were made out of wood and they were flat.

Mother made all of our clothes. My sister and I had two school dresses, a play dress, and a Sunday dress. She also made daddy's shirts, but not his overalls. She made them out of a material called Hickory Stripe. It looked like pillow ticking and was blue and white. She bought it by the bolt. Our underwear was made from sugar sacks and aprons out of feed bags.

We were not sick a lot in our family. When we needed someone, our doctor was called on the phone and came out to the house.

We did not feel safe during the Depression. We had lots of problems with stealing. The corn crib and smoke house were always locked.

I attended a two-room schoolhouse which contained seven grades. We walked two miles to school and this building is still being used today as a parish building for the Lutheran church. Later, we went on into Lexington for our school and rode a school bus. For some reason though, the bus would not come up to our door and we still had to walk a mile before we caught the bus.

My grandfather died in 1933. He was a prominent citizen of the community and was also a Confederate veteran. It was a big funeral and well attended. Our family all lived in the same house.

We felt Roosevelt was a fine President. We listened to his inauguration over the radio at a neighbor's house. The sound was very full of static and it was hard to listen with all of the crackling over the wires."

- KS - South Carolina

.   .   .

"I grew up near the North Carolina border and had a hard time of it when I was young. I had one sister who was younger than me and my father was a sharecropper. Before the Depression, my mother left us. She was only 13 when she married my father, who was very much older than her, and had two children by the time she was 15. It hurt me very much that she chose to leave us and I have never seen her since to find out why she left us alone with father.

When the Depression came, my father tried to keep us together, but he could not find anybody who would buy his crops. My father told me he was sick and could no longer care for us. Then, he dropped us off at a local house.

These people had a farm and six children of their own. In addition to their own children, they were also foster parents to about 15 other children. All of the children were expected to work on the farm and we tended cows, horses, chickens and the crops.

My formal schooling was stopped after I entered the eighth grade. When I was 16, I began farming on my own and moved in with my future wife's family.

My wife was the oldest of six children and she managed a sixth grade education. I lived with her family for two years. In 1939, my wife and I slipped away to get married because her mother did not like me. We made an excuse we were going to the fair and got married that night. We kept our marriage a secret for a couple of weeks.

I farmed on another mans' farm and did not have to pay rent to him for our house. The Depression was not really over for us until I entered the Navy in 1942.

I remember when I was still going to school I saw a dead black man off in the woods one day. I ran to the closest farm and informed the farmer there that a black man had been shot in the head and we needed to do something.

"Son," he said, "It is best you just go on your way and forget what you saw today." Life was hard during those times, and people often disappeared without any traces. Being up in the mountains, there were many people who got away with murder. Other people may have known someone had killed another person but they kept their mouths shut for fear they would be the next one dead or another missing person in the community.

If a person had a still in the woods, it was not uncommon for them to shoot anybody who came close by, and they never had to answer for it either. We had law enforcement, but they were scarce. People were their own law during those times.

My mother-in-law continued to hate me over the years. In fact, she erased my face from all of our family pictures later. As a result, I do not have any pictures of me with my family at all."

- FBC - South Carolina

.   .   .

"I was born in 1930. We lived in a mill town in Laurens, South Carolina and my parents both worked at the mill for $12 a week. We lived in a two bedroom house with a bath that belonged to the mill.

My grandparents were farmers during the Depression. When I was five, they moved in with us. They had to break up housekeeping because nobody had any money to buy their crops.

There were four adults and three children in this small house and it was pretty crowded. We had a few chickens out back of the house, and when my grandparents came, they brought a cow. There was no room in the backyard for the cow and many other families also had cows. So, the mill fenced in a pasture for them at the bottom of the house beside the mill. Twice a day, we would go down the hill which was about 3/4 of a mile from the house, fetch the cow, and bring her up to the yard to be milked.

There was one time I remember when all of us got sick at the same time. The plant nurse would come up from the mill and give us medicines to make us well.

My grandmother made all of our clothes from empty flour sacks. We girls had two dresses. One was for school and one was for church. After church was over on Sunday, we would go home and immediately take our dress off. My father repaired all of our shoes on a regular basis.

We did not celebrate holidays. Christmas was a shoe box filled with fruit and nuts. I did not even taste cake until the family had a reunion. There were about 30 people that came together and they pooled their resources to make the food. One of the members of the family scrounged up enough ingredients to make a cake.

We ate beans, corn bread, biscuits and gravy, and every once in a while had a slab of fat back. We churned and made our own butter. To this day, I still love biscuits and gravy. It is one of my favorite meals.

I remember when I was seven in 1936 my father, who was not a drinker, came home drunk. He mistook an ashtray for a slop jar and peed in the ashtray. I got very scared and cried.

When my father sobered up, my mother told him about how frightened I was of him. My father was very remorseful because he did not want his children to be afraid of him. He turned to religion right after that and was saved."

- BBC - South Carolina

.   .   .

"My father was a farmer. He also did carpentry work if he could find it.

I was the oldest of a large family. There were three girls and three boys.

My mother worked at Burlington Hosiery Mill in Harriman, Tennessee. She earned 50 cents a day. She walked seven miles to the mill in the morning and seven miles back at night. We were so poor she did not even have a pair of shoes. The weather in East Tennessee is often wet or rainy, and in the winter, it snows. The ground is also very rocky and rough so walking barefoot was not an easy task for her.

Because I was the oldest, it became my responsibility to raise my brothers and sisters. By the time I was six, I was cooking all the meals for the whole family. My grandmother made me quit school after the third grade. She felt it was more important for me to take care of the family.

My best memories are of Sunday. We would walk to church in the morning, and then we would go to different people's houses to eat in the afternoon. My father played the fiddle and we would have big dances all that afternoon. This was my only opportunity to play with other kids."

VMB - Tennessee

.   .   .

"I remember I had only overalls to wear and no shirt. I was ashamed and cold. I wore my jacket to school all that day.

I acted up in class and the teacher ordered me to the front of the room for a spanking. When I got there, she made me take off my jacket. After she saw I did not have a shirt, she whacked me a couple of times very softly with the paddle and let me go."

- JPG - Tennessee

.   .   .

"I was born in 1919 in the country between Harriman and Rockwood, Tennessee. The name of the town was Cardiff. There were about 50 people who lived around Cardiff. Most of them were related to each other and everyone knew everybody and their business.

Cardiff consisted of a railroad station stop, a general store and a church. The general store sold everything that was needed from kerosene to bologna.

My father worked for the Tennessee-Southern railroad and had a steady income during the depression. I do not remember any real hardship for money during this time. I had one sister two years younger than me.

All the boys in the area wore overalls. I had three pair. One was for church. My shirts were made out of flour sacks.

I attended a one-room schoolhouse. All the grades were together.

When family died, we did not have the luxury of a funeral home. The family would lay the person out at home. Often, this was in their very own bed.

To get a doctor, you had to be real sick. He came out from the other towns on a horse and buggy.

We walked everywhere we had to go. We even walked the ten miles to visit Harriman. Harriman had a big Fourth Of July celebration. There were free fireworks and they were really something to see.

Birthdays were not celebrated, but I particularly liked Christmas and Thanksgiving. We would gather at one of the relative's houses and there was absolutely everything to eat. It was a big spread of food such as pies and ice cream. I really looked forward to the festivities and enjoyed this time of year very much.

It was a big thing to get something for Christmas that was store-bought. I recall getting a slingshot one year. I was very happy. We also got a piece of fruit and that was basically what we received for Christmas. Some years, I would also get a shirt. It was always homemade and was made out of flour sacks.

When we grew older, we did not like having boys coming from the towns to see "our" girls. We would throw rocks at them or beat them up.

Cardiff had a railroad stop, and as a train came into town, it would slow down. We would hop on the train while it was still moving and steal fruit off the train.

One time one of my cousins got locked in a refrigerator car. He could not get out. We frantically ran to a house and borrowed a car so that we could drive ten miles to the next town and free him. We arrived and got him out, but he was nearly frozen to death by the time we got there.

I only finished the seventh grade. After that, I worked on local farms until I joined the army at age 16.

One time we had a dance at our house. We invited everybody. We did not have to move the furniture because we didn't have any. Our furniture consisted of four chairs, a kitchen table, a couch and three beds. Everybody had a great time."

- JHB - Tennessee

. . .

"Our family lived out in the woods in the Pee Dee region of South Carolina during the Depression. We survived by hunting wild game. Buckshot was cheap in those days and we would hunt, ducks, deer, raccoons, and even opossums. You could say we went after anything that moved in order to have food to eat.

There were people in the area who knew how to clean out the insides of opossums. They were not fit to eat for about a month after you killed them.

One time some Northerners came down to our region, and of course, we had to hunt in order to feed all of them. We caught a lot of opossums and cleaned them out good. Now those Yankees sat down and ate those opossums, but you can bet, I didn't!"

- Mr. J - South Carolina

. . .

"I grew up in North Carolina. In 1928, I was a junior at Columbia College and my father died. When his will was read, there was no money for me until I finished college. It was my plan to go to Europe after school, but by the time I finished college, there was no money to be had because the banks had failed and all of our money was gone.

I taught in a mill school and later in a poor country district. I was paid $55 in script. The banks normally charged ten percent to cash the script note, but my father had had connections with a bank in Virginia that gave me all of my money.

I was an only child and my middle name is Only. My parents were also only children, and I fell in love at age 25 with a young man who was also an only child.

19

I lived at home with my mother in St. Stephens and it was seven long years before my husband and I could afford to get married.

We married in 1934 in a small, old church. It was decorated by my many friends who picked wild flowers from a ditch near the road. My mother gave me away. The times were hard and we persevered and grew spiritually because of our hardships.

I was outgoing and my husband was an introvert. I was more impulsive and extroverted while he was shy and a perfectionist. We were married for 47 years and it is my opinion that marriages are made here on this earth rather than in heaven. We looked out at the world in our relationship and did not spend much time looking inward at ourselves. We too had only one child and when he grew up he had one child, too. So, a pattern was set in our family.

We were surrounded by poverty in Berkley County and our family met many other people's needs. The table was always well set, and I have no favorites or dislikes in food. I eat food to live. I do not enjoy food for food's sake.

We shared with other people and fed others besides ourselves. I do not recall us ever discussing money during these times. When a need came up, God always provided.

If my schoolchildren were sick, I had doctor friends I called on to help. If someone died and there was not enough money for a shroud, we would pool our resources to meet the need."

EOL - South Carolina

.   .   .

"I was born in 1911 in Columbia, South Carolina. I was the youngest of seven children.

When the Depression came in 1929, I was attending Hollings College near Roanoke, Virginia. Our class was affected hard by the Depression and I remember at least nine that did not make it back the following year. Our class originally started with 127 students but only 60 of us graduated. My mother died during my junior year in college.

I graduated with a B.A. Degree in History. Then, I got my Masters.

In 1932, I got a job teaching high school in Greenwood, South Carolina. My salary that year was $791.50 and I taught English and General Science. Although I did not get paid for it, I also coached the girls basketball team.

The Depression really hit in 1933-34. I was only paid for two months in the fall and received no more money until June at the end of the school year and then it was in script. I cashed the script in for 95 cents on the dollar. My father helped me out during this time. It was the only way I could make it.

I moved to Anderson in 1934 and was able to teach history. I earned $900 and taught there until 1937. I moved to Columbia in 1937 and made $1100 and $1200 the following year.

I do not recall having a bad time during the Depression. I had food to eat and clothes to wear, but there was no money ever for extras. I even was able to afford a train ride to visit one of my brothers and attended the Chicago World's Fair.

My father was a doctor in Columbia. During his career as a General Practitioner, he delivered 7,000 babies. My father made out all of his own bills. If a man had five children he was struggling to raise, my father would often send him a bill for only half of what he owed. He charged $2.00 for an office visit and $3.00 for a house call all through his career.

My father felt you had to have a calling to work in medicine. He often said that if you wanted to make lots of money you needed to choose another profession.

He died in the 1940's and was greatly loved by his patients. They had a portrait made of him and it is now in the Hall of Fame at Richland Memorial Hospital. His name was James H. McIntosh.

At our house, we had a Negro named Sam who lived with us. He had originally joined the family to be my father's buggy boy when he started his practice. Sam stayed with us and was a member of our family for many years. I was told once by Sam that a tramp had heard about our house all the way in Florida. We never turned anyone away. They always got food.

People have often said to me that I must have been spoiled by being the youngest of seven children. I reply that I had a lot of bosses. If I was spoiled, it was in one way. Sunday dinner was always fried chicken. It did not matter where we were, I always got the pulley bone!

I adored Roosevelt as President. He was an inspiring man. I have only voted for one Republican all my life."

- NP - South Carolina

.   .   .

"I graduated from high school in 1932 and immediately joined the Civilian Conservation Corps. The CCC was created by President Roosevelt to provide work for young men ages 18 to 25.

We were allowed to be in the Civilian Conservation Corps for only one year. During this time, we built state parks, fire towers,. telephone lines to connect the towers, and trails for fire containment. At that time, there were no Federally owned lands and most of the work we did was on private land. The camp where I worked was in Walterboro and there were a total of 15 camps in the state.

The Corps personnel were controlled by the army and our life was very much like that of the army. The Forest Service administered the projects. We lived in tents and rose at 5:30 a.m., ate breakfast, and then, went to work. Our day ended around 5:00 p.m., and we ate supper and then went on to bed.

We were paid $1.00 a day. It was a rule of the CCC that $25 a month was sent to your parents. I was only allowed to keep $5.00 of my pay and I spent it. I recall cokes cost five cents (six cents when you added the penny tax) and cigarettes were 15 cents.

There were 200 people in the camp and they were all males. Sometimes on the weekends we had bands for entertainment, but you couldn't do much on $5 a month.

The reason why I joined the CCC was because I was hungry and without a job. My father was a Russian immigrant who worked as a tailor, but he became ill during the Depression. I became the sole support for my parents and my two younger brothers. The CCC provided clothes, food, and a place to sleep for me, and helped my family through this difficult time.

My memory of the Depression was that life was very difficult for me, but everybody was having a hard time.

After my year in the CCC, I returned to Columbia and worked at various jobs until I went into the army in 1940. My father never did regain his health and died in the late 1930's.

I greatly loved and respected President Roosevelt. He was fabulous, and to me, he was the greatest man who ever served as President. He was a genius and a true leader. I thank God for his foresight. He saved me, my family, and many of my contemporaries."

- PG - South Carolina

· · ·

"I was born in 1914 in Georgia. I was the oldest of six children. Two were boys and four were girls.

My father worked for the railroad, but lost his job in 1932. The railroad wanted the house back and we moved to Cataula, Georgia.

My mother's parents had a 100-acre farm there with a dilapidated house on it. The house had no electricity, no telephone, and no indoor plumbing. However, we didn't feel this was uncommon.

My father's parents also did not live far away and my grandfather worked as a pumper for the railroad. He helped us get seed and equipment to run the farm. My father was ill and I worked the farm by myself for about one and one-half years. For money, we sawed wood.

In October, 1933, I joined the Civilian Conservation Corps. I went to their base in Ft. Benning, Georgia for training. Then, I went to Albany, Georgia where we fought fires, made fire breaks, and put up telephone lines.

The CCC was formed for young men ages 17 to 25 and you were only eligible to serve for one year, but I stayed on longer than that. After six months at Albany, I asked for a transfer to Warm Springs, Georgia.

Warm Springs was FDR's pet project. He stayed there more than he was in Washington, and it was called the Little White House.

We had drill every Saturday morning, and I was consistently judged to be one of the best. In 1934, five to six of us were asked to be guards at FDR's Thanksgiving dinner. I stood outside one of the windows while about 40 people ate dinner at Warm Springs. It was a honorary thing to be chosen as guard and I do not recall all who were there.

Roosevelt was crippled with polio and he could not walk without the aid of sticks. I recall he always traveled by train. He was a very impressive and outstanding man. He had a wonderful voice and appearance and was a very warm and caring person.

In 1935, a CCC camp was established in Pine Mountain, Georgia. I was still in the CCC and had become a supply Sargent. I earned $45 a month of which $25 was sent to my parents. I was very happy in the CCC. I was young, ambitious, and hardworking and received several promotions.

I met my future wife in Pine Mountain. I saw her in choir at church one day. When we dated, we went to church, rode around into the country and held hands, and every once in a while went to a movie. We even went to Manchester once because I had won a 50- cent prize at the movies. For recreation, we would walk three blocks uptown and get two hamburgers and two drinks for 20 cents at Krystal. Then, we would go to the movies for 15 cents each.

I left the CCC and worked as a salesman in a general merchandise store that sold feed and other goods. I got the job for less money than I was making at the camp.

During the Depression, you took whatever work you could get. No one could afford to be picky about a job. It was not until World War II before I got a job in electrical work which was what I had trained to do in school.

People bartered and traded for what they needed in the Depression. If someone came into to the store with eggs or corn, we would take that and then they would get their goods at ten percent difference.

Eggs sold for ten cents a dozen. If you could find bread, it was five cents a loaf. To find bread however was like buying a piece of cake.

In 1937, I went to Macon, Georgia to work at Swift Company. They were a branch house of the meat packing business. I began working in shipping and receiving and later was promoted to beef cutter. I worked 10 to 16 hours a day and made $17.50 a week.

My wife and I were also married in 1937. We were married in her parent's living room. We caught the afternoon train back to Macon on a Saturday. I had found an apartment for us, but later we found out it was in a bad neighborhood. We moved a few months later.

We would get our groceries in a wheelbarrow and five gallons of kerosene for $5.00. Our apartment was one bedroom and a kitchen. The bath was shared with four other people.

Other memories I have was that the WPA was formed by Roosevelt for unemployed adults. The cities were where the real suffering was and the people there benefited from this program.

I also recall nigras would chop down pine trees and make charcoal from them. It was 12 miles to Columbus and they would leave on Friday night with their load and not get back until Sunday afternoon. The charcoal was used to heat irons and they would sell to the people who did the washing in the city.

We had lots of family get-togethers and we lived a fair distance apart. I recall the roads weren't paved and we would often get four to five punctures in the tires before we got home from these gatherings.

The FDR administration also bought a strip of land between Pine Mountain and Hamilton. It was called Pine Mountain Valley and was subdivided into 20-acre farms with a house on it. City people were paid $40 subsistence to move there.

I was a young man during this time and was opposed to Social Security. I did not like the idea of the government taking charge of our affairs. Now, my wife and I wonder if we will be receiving any money at all next year because of current talk in Congress.

Two of my sisters went on to college and got their teaching degrees. Two of my other sisters went onto business school, and my brother worked for the railroad."

- CO - Georgia

· · ·

"My parents owned a farm about one mile out from Pine Mountain, Georgia. I was the oldest of four children and was eleven years-old when the Depression began.

My father had a dairy farm in addition to our farm, also. He sold his milk for five cents a quart. Daddy used 2 to 12 back people to help with the farm, and in the summertime, we helped, too.

I recall daddy gave almost as much away of his farm goods as he kept. People did not have any money, and he couldn't get paid. We almost went broke.

We basically raised everything we needed except for sugar, flour, and coffee. We had a Sunday dress and mother made our clothes. We had enough, but not too much.

When illness came, my mother made a peach leaf poultice that took care of infections. I do not recall us ever going to the doctor.

People also came to the farm to get our produce. Mother would put the money she got from them in a tin can. We always knew the money was there for us, but we had to have a special purpose to use it.

We sold chickens for fifty cents. These were chickens that had been killed, plucked, and cleaned. Mother would take this money and save it. She earned enough to buy my brother his graduation suit. It was very beautiful and we were all proud.

We were lucky. My brother now lives on the farm our parents owned."

- BO - Georgia

.   .   .

"In 1929, when the bottom dropped out on Wall Street, it was not such a blow to my family because my father worked for the city. We also had no savings when the banks failed and it did not affect us too much either. We were poor, but I didn't realize it.

I had three older brothers and they all worked at any kind of job they could find. My mother sewed and made all of my clothes. She was also a wonderful manager so we survived.

In 1935, I finished high school and my mother had saved $100 from grocery money. She offered it to me to attend the local college in Charleston, South Carolina. I started college with four home-made dresses. I had to get a job at the playground in order to finish college.

One of the things I remember was my father was paid in "Script" money for a year. We went to buy me a new pair of shoes and the cost was $4.50. We only had "Script" money for $5.00 so we did not get any change.

The happiest Christmas I ever had in those days was the one when I received a large rubber ball and a pleated skirt. The ball had red and blue stripes and large bumps on it. I played a game with it on my front steps and I made my own rules.

My younger brother and I played on the city playgrounds. It did not cost a cent to play and we stayed out of trouble.

I was in a girl's club during high school. There were ten of us and at Christmas we exchanged gifts. You could not pay over ten cents for any one gift. Some of the things that ten cents bought were tangee lipstick, a small package of bobby pins, note paper pads, a small package of writing paper, and two packages of Life Savers. We thought they were great!

My father was a staunch democrat. He loved President Roosevelt."

- EJL - South Carolina

.   .   .

"Most people do not realize that if it had not been for the WPA our cities would not have the water and sewage systems they have today. The WPA also gave out-of-work men their dignity by having them work with picks and shovels on these projects for the little pay they received. There were no handouts, like there are today, in the 1930's. If you did not work, you did not eat. The WPA provided honest work while keeping a man's dignity and for this Roosevelt was a genius. We should have more people working today for their assistance.

Our town of Anderson was struck by a tornado in the 1930;s without any warning. I was playing ball in the street with friends. Mr. Boggs, a next-door neighbor, had seen the black cloud coming in from the west. He came out of his house and yelled, 'You boys get home now and tell your parents to lock up.' We just looked at him because we had been playing hard and were not paying attention to the weather.

He shouted at us again, 'Get home Now! There's a tornado coming.' We looked in the direction he was pointing and then ran home as fast as we could.

We all got safely inside, except for Mr. Boggs. He had just put his hands on his back door when it hit. The winds blew him away from his house and rolled him into the wire of his chicken coup. It was a furious storm that only lasted a few minutes. Mr. Boggs survived with scratches and bruises. We all felt it was a miracle he survived."

- South Carolina

.   .   .

"I was born in South Carolina and have resided here all my life. In retrospect, I realize more and more that the 1930's were great years for me when I was a teenager and college-age child. Our family consisted of six children who were born within a span of eight years. Truly, my parents must have faced many problems making ends meet. However, we children never felt the real stresses of the times.

None of our friends lived a plush lifestyle so we were satisfied to have only a few toys and to mend them if they broke, to resew baseballs, to restring tennis rackets, or even to use old newspapers, flour glue, and limbs from shrubs to make us good kites. The tail of the kite was a strip of cloth from an old sheet. All such fun, or so we thought!

I recall cutting paper dolls from an old Sears-Roebuck catalog. I also sewed doll clothes from scraps left from our homemade dresses. This proved to be fun for us and our friends.

Passing down clothes was sometimes done and I loved anticipating getting items from my three older sisters which they had outgrown. We all got one nice, new Sunday outfit and we knew when we returned from church or a dress-up occasion to carefully put that outfit in our closet to use again.

I vividly recall the closeness of my family. We had happiness with even limited resources. My parents were both persons of strong faith and we children were blessed to grow up in a Christian home with the right values.

After A.A. and church services, we had a family meal at home. There were eight at the table and we shared not only a good meal, but lots of good conversations, too. Sunday dinner was usually fried chicken, rice and gravy, fresh vegetables, biscuits and a dessert of pie or cake and maybe ice cream.

No allowances were given at my home, but we were given money for our needs. For a while, I was delighted to receive one dollar for a day's work at the local Five and Ten Cents store. It was good pay then!

Birthdays and holidays were usually family gatherings if such was possible. However, the years we were in college (four of us for five years straight), we usually came home only at Christmas and at the end of the year. We traveled by train because we had only one car for our family of eight. Young people had no cars of their own. Gifts at Christmas and on birthdays were usually items to wear.

Some of the happiest times we had in the 1930's were during holidays when my parents took us to see interesting places in the United States. These trips were by train. We observed lots from the train windows before we reached our destinations.

My family was blessed with very little illness. Parental doctoring was usually the order of the day. Nearly all childhood illnesses could be cured with castor oil, Vick's salve, cough syrup, chest clothes, iodine and antiseptic powder for wounds, and a strip torn from a clean white sheet to bandage any wound seemed all we needed. Home-made chicken soup seemed best to help us snap back. We found doctors were not often needed, and when one was needed to prescribe often it could be done by telephone.

I was quite aware of tramps coming into our town. They hanged onto freight trains or rode in empty box cars. They roamed the streets looking for a bit of work or a good meal which my mother was proud to give. I dreaded to go the door when I knew one of these loners was there. Sometimes one had small tools and wanted to repair broken umbrellas or even repair pots and pans.

In the 1930's, Roosevelt's New Deal seemed the solution to our problems and many of its programs did help greatly. However, "Let the government do it" philosophy caught fire and laziness and lack of family responsibility became so universal that today we are still bogged down in welfare. Present day generations could not stand a repeat of the 1930's!

To summarize: I am sure my parents shielded us children from the realities of the 1930's because they desired that we all have a happy childhood experience. We all pulled together, had faith, and respected our parents and appreciated what they did for us. Things were not so important for us in the 1930's so my memories are of fun-filled years!"

- LDC - South Carolina

• • •

"I went to college in 1930 and graduated in 1934. I remember my mother helping others. Tramps knew they could always get a meal at our house. Mother fed many of them on our back steps.

Mother had a big garden and she loved to cook. A little black boy came to our house late each afternoon and mother sent home a pot of leftovers to his family. This black mother told a friend of ours that Mother kept them from starving during this time.

I don't remember much about clothes. Mother made them. There didn't seem to be much money, but my parents were good managers. We must have been very lucky. I always felt loved and protected. We lived in a small town in South Carolina."

- South Carolina

• • •

"I was born in June, 1925. These are my most vivid memories of life in Charleston, South Carolina during the 1930's. I remember getting up before the rest of the family and walking half a block to the corner of Broad & Rutledge. I waited for the seven o'clock trolley so that I could greet our cook.

I remember going to Moultrie playground to watch softball on warm summer nights. This was a favorite pastime because not many people had extra money to have an evening out on the town.

I remember we had a ice box and watching the ice wagon come by daily was exciting. It was wonderful to hop up on the back and grab a sliver of ice.

Movies were ten cents. Milk was 15 cents a quart and bread was ten cents.

Cars would ride on Folly Beach, and on Sunday afternoon, we would drive to the beach and bathe in the surf. The cars had shades to pull down on the windows and we would undress in the car. My parents would not go in the surf, but they allowed us to go in and watched us from the beach."

- ES - South Carolina

• • •

"I was a very young child during the Depression years. My father worked for the power company in Charleston, South Carolina so I do not recall us ever having a hard time of it.

I do remember a tornado coming through in 1937 and it destroyed the slave market. Later, there was also a big fire down at the docks.

I recall getting spanked at least once a week. My mother spanked me for things I did and I did not do. If my father came home and mother had not yet finished with my spanking, he would take it up for her. Parents did not spare the rod on children like they do today.

One time, I got a spanking for letting my younger brother fall into the creek. Another time my mother received a bill for a bag of candy from the grocery store. In those days, you could go to the store and put things on a charge account and then settle the bill once a month. Mother asked me if I had gotten the candy. I said, "No." Then we went to the owner of the store and he said, "Yes, he got the candy." My mother spanked me hard for this. Then, years later when it did not matter anymore, my younger brother admitted he was the one who had gotten the candy that day!"

- DD - South Carolina

.   .   .

"My father had ten children by two wives. He was officially a farmer in Lake City, but could not make a decent living by just farming for his large family. So, he made liquor, too.

He didn't try to hide his still and he was never caught moonshining. His still was off in the woods under a big water oak tree. He would run the still late at night and the oak tree would disperse the smoke.

He had no competition in the area he served. There was an understanding he was the only moonshiner for the area. He covered Georgetown, Hemingway, Johnsonville, and Lake City.

He was very popular and delivered his liquor in a Model T pick-up with a tobacco sheet covering his jugs. He never returned from a trip with anything left in his truck.

The revenuers kept track of who bought large quantities of jugs in the area. Because of this, he had an understanding with his customers that if you bought a jug you had to give him one back in return.

He did a lot of trading. He traded for land, pigs, and trucks. His dresser drawer in the bedroom would often been jammed full of money, but he would only spend for necessities. He lived a simple life. Although he made lots of money, it was squandered or lost by the time he died.

There was a family who owned a store in town that gouged people by raising prices on things to people who could not afford anything. My father avoided these people and went to the other side of town to do business because they had made a fortune by cheating poor people. He felt this was very wrong."

- HN - South Carolina

.   .   .

Our family lived near Georgetown on the Lynches River. My father horse-traded for things that we needed. He also caught fish on the river. He caught catfish, shad, and roe herring. The herring and shad were caught by using chicken wire. However, the family did not live off the fish. He would sell them for the staples we needed instead.

My father also carved things that were needed. He had a one-handed carving tool and made a bathtub and cooking bowls.

Our family grew out of our existing home and we needed a larger house. It took daddy one week to cut the trees off our land, one week to cut it at the lumber mill, and one week to build the house. We could not afford windows at the time so we lived without windows for one year.

We always had a garden, and we dug our own well."

- South Carolina

•   •   •

My father was raised in Wilson, North Carolina. He was a farmer and a bootlegger. He had four children.

The revenuers and lawmen were pretty smart about illegal whiskey making and he had to hide his still. It was located in the top of his tobacco barn. He covered up his operation by having tobacco in the barn during the summer and having sweet potatoes, which had to have heat, in the winter.

He drove around to his customers in the oldest, raggedyest truck he could find.

When they had a load to take up north, he would have a layer of watermelons sitting on top. Right underneath all the melons was where the liquor was hidden.

He made a lot of money, but always said, 'Son, don't flaunt that you got money. If you feel you have to flaunt or brag about it, do it at home.'"

- HW - North Carolina

•   •   •

"I was born in South Carolina and my most vivid memory is of my mother working away from home. My saddest moment during the Depression was when my grandfather died and my happiest moment was graduating from high school.

When family became ill, I would help nurse them. We paid for personal goods with cash money, and if gifts were received at Christmas, they were usually new clothes. My family has always had the church be a large part in their lives.

My favorite meal was pork chops. My least favorite meal was okra or cabbage.

My impression of Roosevelt as president was that he was a savior of our country."

- ED - South Carolina

•   •   •

"At the time of the Depression, I was living in Roanoke County, Virginia. I was nine years old in 1929.

My most vivid memory was of a visit to my cousin's home by two women from St. Louis (her sisters-in-law). I recall listening to them describe living through a summer of intense heat, a drought, and the dust bowl.

This was at the same time we were experiencing a drought and our big vegetable garden that had always been so lush and productive withered and died. We depended on it for all our meals and always gave lots to relatives in the city. My mother had such a hard time that summer. Lots of time for supper, we only ate biscuits and scrambled eggs.

One of my saddest movements came when one of our classmates died. The church and graveyard were right beside the school grounds. We watched the mourners at the burial from the second story windows. All the family wore black.

I remember my childhood and teen years as a happy time - always. We had a big house and farm and lots of relatives and friends who visited often. We had horses to ride and a mountain to climb.

My parents were well-educated and smart. They kept up with current events. They liked to talk politics. My mother kept the radio on in the kitchen all day long.

One of my mother's brothers lost his job and the whole family (five of them) moved in with us for the summer. My sisters and I were not too happy about that because we had to rearrange our living quarters.

Even though we were two miles off the main highway, many tramps came to our home asking for food. I remember one who had seven hats stacked up on his head. My mother always took the children upstairs and my father and grandmother fed the tramps. The train track ran by my aunt's home and we saw many hoboes riding in the box cars. We used to stand out in her yard just to watch for them.

My mother made a special day of each birthday. I never had a birthday party (they weren't so fashionable then), and the only present I received was always a five dollar bill from my aunt for whom I was named. One of our neighbors, who was my mother's close friends, always decorated a beautiful cake for our birthdays.

For Christmas, I received two gifts. I recall once getting a string of beads, once a glass basket (depression glass), an ice tea set with pitcher and glasses, and once a ceramic couch. I still have them on display in my home.

We had a big breakfast on Christmas morning. It included a caramel cake which was my father's favorite. Mother always had a special centerpiece for the big table in the kitchen. The one I remember most vividly was a large round pan filled with sawdust. In the sawdust, she had stuck 100 small red candles. She lit all of them just as we sat down to eat.

The only time we had oranges and nuts was for Christmas. We literally lived off the land and bought only things like rice, sugar, tea, coffee and cheese.

As I mentioned before, the only money I ever got was the birthday money. I horded it and would charge interest to a brother or a sister who borrowed from me.

A seamstress would come from town in late summer and stay at our house to make school dresses. The rest of our clothes were ordered from the Sears-Roebuck catalog - even hats.

The only time I remember going to a movie was to see Lionel Barrymore in the "Lion and the Mouse." We went because it was the first movie with sound to come to Roanoke.

My parents were Democrats. Father was a member of the County Democratic Committee. Of course, they, like all other Democrats, were supportive of Roosevelt. We listened to all of his fireside chats on the radio and had Roosevelt's picture on a shelf in the kitchen.

For the dedication of the VA Hospital in Roanoke County, Roosevelt came to speak. I still remember vividly the shock of seeing him pushed up on the platform in a wheelchair. He had such a strong, wonderful voice and he looked so vigorous in the photographs that I did not realize he was crippled. Our whole family took the day off and sat around the Philco radio for each inauguration.

Not once in my lifetime can I remember my parents or grandparents losing faith because of anything that happened. My older sister once said, 'It was not blind faith either.' We were read stories from the bible every Sunday night until we were grown. We all attended church regularly, prayed and read our bibles."

- MWS - Virginia

.　　.　　.

"My life was greatly affected by the Depression years of the 1930's in South Carolina.

I finished high school in June, 1931. I was eager to attend Winthrop College. My parents told me they could not afford to send me to college. I tried out and got a County scholarship. I borrowed money to make up the rest. My parents contributed what they could. I was able to finish college in June, 1935 and taught Home Economics for forty years.

During these years, my father had to mortgage our farm. My younger brother worked his way through the University of South Carolina, and I paid off the mortgage after I finished college.

We raised most of our own food on the farm. These were fruits, vegetables, and meats. With the little available money, we bought enough staples to get by. We ate well. My parents sold farms products - butter, cream, eggs, vegetables, fruits, and meats - to have a little cash on hand.

We celebrated holidays by getting together with our families for meals and picnics. Our main gifts were clothes, fruits, and a few toys which we tried to take good care of. I still have my doll carriage and bed which were given to me before the Depression years.

If any one of our family members became ill, we looked after each other. Our aunts and cousins would help us.

My father worked as a foreman on road project (the W.P.A.) during the Depression to get a little extra to help with the income from the farm. Farm prices were very low.

Living near a state highway, we helped many strangers with food as they walked the roads hunting for jobs.

We were glad to get hand-me-down clothes from older members of the family when they grew out of their clothes. My mother and I sewed many of our clothes, too.

We were active Church members. We did not lose faith. We had to walk a mile each Sunday to get a ride with an uncle to church because our T-Model Ford had given out. The church and school meant much to us during these days.

Times were hard, but now I am glad I lived through the Depression because I can now appreciate everything I have because I had to work for it.

I feel that Roosevelt was a great President. He helped to get us through the Depression years.

One of my saddest moments was seeing my parents always doing without so we children could have things.

One of my happiest moments was graduation from college and getting a job. They were also scarce.

I worked 40 years straight and have been retired 20 years."

- MRD - South Carolina

.   .   .

"I do not remember having a hard time growing up during the Depression. My father was employed by Mead and I do not remember any money worries.

My mother was an excellent seamstress. She would walk downtown, look at the fashions in the store, and then return home and duplicate it.

I also remember we moved several times. However, we always stayed in the same general area.

My favorite pastime was playing with paper dolls. I would cut fashion pictures out from the Sears Roebuck catalog to use for my doll dresses. I would spend many happy hours changing my dolls' wardrobes."

- EW - Tennessee

.   .   .

"I was born in 1908 and lived in Rhoda, Virginia in a coal mining camp as a young bride with my husband and mother. We had five children - four boys and one girl.

The coal company owned our houses, ran the commissary, and provided the doctor. We were paid in script and 75 cents of script bought a dollar's worth of goods at the general store (commissary).

We did all of our own sewing. We would make dish towels out of flour and sugar sacks. We had our own chickens and I served chicken twice a week. We also had soup beans a lot. I did not like fish. We were always concerned about the bones in them for the children.

Birthdays were a family dinner. We did not exchange gifts at Christmas.

Our house rental was $6.50 a month. Shoes were $2.99.

My favorite holiday was July Fourth. One of my four sons was born on this day. It was a day of flags, ice cream, watermelons, and a family reunion.

My husband worked in the coal mine and also had a shoe shop. In 1931, I wanted him out of the mines so he began painting the houses for the coal company.

My children were born at home. We would call in a neighbor lady to come to help out. The doctor would sit and read until I hollered and said it was time he got up and did something.

My husband and I were both born into large families. We each had six brothers and sisters.

- MC - Virginia

•   •   •

"I grew up in a small coal-mining community in Southwest Virginia. My father worked in a wholesale hardware store selling primarily coal-mining equipment.

My paternal grandmother lived in the same town. We owned our own house which was heated by a coal-burning stove in the living room and the coal cook stove.

We were poor, but so was everyone else in the town. Because of this, we didn't feel 'disadvantaged.'

Our school was surprisingly good. I was awarded a partial scholarship to college upon graduation. Later, my brother qualified for the Navy V-12 program.

I had acute appendicitis when I was ten. I was in the local hospital for the operation. I am sure this was expensive, but I do not recall this being mentioned."

- VC - Virginia

•   •   •

"I recall people did not have any money during the Depression. In order to get what we needed, we traded for everything. I remember taking eggs to the store and I would trade them for thread my mother needed for sewing.

Our family had about 75 acres in Saluda County. We had a pair of mules and raised crops for our own and our animals' needs.

My father supplied eggs around the area. He also had a press and would press sugar cane into syrup for people. He would keep a portion of the syrup as payment.

There were no locked doors in our community. In the summer months, all the windows and the doors would stay wide open in order to catch the breeze.

There not not many paved roads during the 1930's in South Carolina. If it rained and you went out afterwards, it was just a matter of time before you got stuck. Then, people would come out and help you out. That was what the 1930's was about - people helping each other out.

There were also many flat tires with no spares. You stopped and patched the tire right on the road.

I do not recall having a hard time during these years, but I do remember that you always fed people who came knocking on your door.

Our family was not very political. However, many of my older cousins worked for the CCC during the 1930's. They all thought Roosevelt was a great president, and on the day he died, there was much sadness in our midst."

- ARA - South Carolina

.   .   .

"My parents were farmers in a rural county in Virginia. Right before the Depression, my father lost his farm. He was an ambitious man and he rented land from family members when this happened.

I was one of five children and was eleven years old when the 1930's began. Farmers were self-sustaining. We grew tobacco, corn, and wheat. We went to the mill and ground our own flour and used a grist mill for corn meal and feed for the animals. Our animals were chickens, a cow, pigs, and mules.

When cold weather came in the fall, we would slaughter the hogs. There was no refrigeration and the meat was smoked, salted, and cured. We rarely ever got to eat ham because these were sold for money at Christmas.

We only had one cow which took care of our family needs, but I recall other families would sell the cream off their milk. If someone had many cows, they would make butter to sell.

We would gather eggs and trade them for items we needed at the country store.

Hucksters also visited us. They came out with cages and crates and would buy our young chickens.

In 1934, we were living on the Patrick Henry estate. My father was raising corn. He also worked on a WPA project to build a boulevard in the area. My father was a proud man and he felt Roosevelt provided him with a way to work with honor. My father would not take any handouts. Many families in the area were helped by Roosevelt and this important project.

We had a car, but could not afford to run it. As a result, we used the wagon to get around. I recall I used to be very embarrassed when cars of other families passed us by. I was aware we were poor.

Church was our social life. The women tithed religiously. In the afternoons, we would have fellowship on the ground. We played games, but rarely every any ball. My grandfather did not approve of this game.

We lived far out in the country. Our church shared pastors and we had preaching twice a month. Because we lived 40 miles from town, the preacher would spend the weekend with the families. He was paid with hams and farm goods. This way he could either feed his family or sell our goods to others when he returned to town.

My older brother had a knack for making all kinds of things from scrap he found on the farm. I recall wagons and carts in particular.

We did not celebrate any holidays, except Christmas. The whole week was spent eating and eating and eating at different family members' homes. It hurt my father that he did not have money for things for us. He loved to play Santa Claus. We got one present, and it was a dime store item or something homemade. I remember the ladies took great pride in who could make the prettiest apron.

My mother was thrifty. We did everything ourselves. Nothing was done professionally. She made all our clothes and cut our hair.

All of we children were born at home. When we were babies, we were placed under a shade tree in the fields. As a row was finished, the mother would tend to the baby at the end of the row. When we were small, we were put to work and carried water. As we grew older, we pulled suckers off the tobacco. I did not like this job. The older children would take the leaves and place them on sticks.

We were poor, but most other people were too. However, I was very conscious of people who had more.

Three of my mother's cousins were schoolteachers and had cars. They would pass on their old clothes to my mother. She was a very good seamstress and altered these outfits for me. I was always well-dressed for school.

My father died on the WPA project in 1934. My mother was widowed at age 38 and had two babies, aged one and two, when he died. We moved to one of her brother's farms and the family helped her manage it. My mother's brothers were very good at helping us out.

I recall mother really looked forward to getting a 'Due Bill' from the store. This meant she had credit she could use for the family's needs.

I also remember being frightened when peddlers came by. I was fascinated by their cases which were full of spices and other things.

We traveled many, many miles to got to an accredited high school. We even passed another high school on the way, but my mother wanted us to go on to college. Because of this, we had to attend an accredited school.

High school was easy for my older brother. He never studies as hard as I did. We both got scholarships for college, but he returned after the first semester because he had too much freedom and did not study as he should have done.

I was Valedictorian of my class of twenty. When I went to college, I rode on a train. It was 80 miles from home, but it may as well have been in California because I only returned home at Christmas.

It took two years then to get a professional teaching certificate. In the fall of 1937, I began to teach school in a two-room rural schoolhouse. We had an outdoor toilet, and the teacher's responsibilities were to make the fires at the school, too.

I taught Fourth through Seventh grade and made $70 plus $10 for being Principal. I taught there two years and then returned closer to home. My uncle gave me a car when I returned! I felt I really had it made.

My most painful memory was one year when my father sold some tobacco to buy me some shoes. The fashion that year were laces ups with blunt toed. My father bought me shoes with pointed toes! I was so embarrassed that I wore overshoes to cover them up!

I have always felt the Democrats helped the common people more than any other party. Franklin D. Roosevelt gave people a way to help themselves in the 1930's and still keep their pride and dignity."

- MP - Virginia

.   .   .

"The only time I ever saw my father cry was when the banks failed and he lost all his money."

- South Carolina

.   .   .

"It was the depth of the Depression in 1933, and it was a week before my high school graduation. My young aunt walked the half mile to our house to bring me a gift. "Here is a quarter," she said, "to get your hair fixed."

I was choked with feeling that I could hardly say, "Thank you." I was remembering the grim and unloving stepfather who had made her drop out of school and go to work in the nearby cotton mill in Greenville, South Carolina. I think that she did not finish the seventh grade.

I remembered stepping into this mill and being stunned and cowed by the cotton flying in the air and by the heavy clank of all the machinery. I remembered standing on a hill above this mill the year before in 1932 and seeing a ring of armed National Guardsmen, sent by the governor, setting up tents. The governor had sent them to break the strike against unhealthful conditions, poor pay, and child labor. This aunt's brother-in-law was fired by this mill for striking, but he managed to get a job with the more humane Springs Mills in Lancaster.

My aunt gave me this money out of the tiny paycheck she got from that mill. I knew she was proud of her nieces and nephews who were going on to school, and she wanted me to be what she could never be. She also wanted my hair to be as beautiful as possible for the highly respected event of graduation.

Thank you again, Aunt Eva. You have helped me stay sensitive to all unfairness to all working people, and I am keenly aware of generosity wherever and whenever it is shown."

- V Thomas - South Carolina

•   •   •

"The Great Depression for my family on a farm in rural Alabama was a time of barely eking out a livelihood. The poverty was excruciating, and in retrospect, unbelievable.

Early in the 1930's, my brother had to haul wood to our high school in town to pay for his tuitions, and even though he had a scholarship, he could not afford to go on to college.

By the time I was a senior in high school in 1938, FDR's programs were giving the farmers a ray of hope that times were getting better. I longed to go to college! The only possibility was for me to go to a state teachers college where there was reasonable tuition and there was only training for elementary teachers. For me, there was no choice of college or of a course of study. This limited opportunity would be available if I could find a way to earn expenses. I lived near Alabama Polytechnic Institute and my heart's desire was to study home economics there.

My application was sent to Jacksonville State Teachers College in Jacksonville, Alabama, early in the spring of 1938. I marvel now that I had the nerve to think that my family could provide any assistance even if I were employed at the college. I had no skills with which to bargain except I noted on my application that I could play the piano. With very little formal training in music, how unlikely it would be for that tidbit to mean anything!

While I anxiously awaited a response from JSTC, I placed hope against hope that notification would come that there was a job for me. To my chagrin, a long-awaited reply was negative. There was no work on campus! Furthermore, the only employment available in my home county was factory and farm work. My future looked bleak!

During the summer, the decision was made that I would go back to high school in September to study commercial subjects: shorthand, typing, and bookkeeping. Then, perhaps I could qualify for clerical work of some kind. This plan offered more hope than any alternative. Of course, now I know that I could have gone to a city to 'seek my fortune', but then I was too shy to even dream of such daring.

In September, I rode the bus back to high school with a heavy heart but also with determination to make the best of the situation. My classmates were all gone, and I did not belong to a class. The days were long.

After just one week of classes, I was stunned to see a group of teachers drive up to our farm-house late one afternoon. I wondered what was wrong? Something drastic must have happened to bring these ladies to my house! Imagine what a great sigh of relief there was when I learned that they had brought good news to me!

Since we had no telephones, the college had called my high school principal. They asked him to get the message to me that there was a job for me at JSTC. Why had they called? Because I could play the piano!

My father said that we might be able to manage somehow if the job was in the dorm that cost 15.00 a month for room and board. There was no way that I, a seventeen-year old, could understand what hardship even this concession presented to my parents.

The next day, I went to my principal's office to respond to JSTC. I had never talked on a telephone before and was petrified at the idea that I might have to make the phone call myself. My kind principal, Mr. J. M. Briscoe, made the call the find out in which dorm the work was available. He held the phone while he relayed to me the message that the dorm was a more expensive one than the one to which my father had agreed. I sadly replied, "Then tell them that I cannot accept."

Mr. Briscoe said to me, 'Go! If you go, you will find a way to stay. Let me tell them that you will come.'

Those are the words that changed my life! He was going against my father's wishes in order to give me the encouragement I needed. How grateful I am to him for giving me 'a shove' in the right direction! How grateful I am for the sacrifices that my mother and father made to get me to college and keep me there for the necessary two years for teacher certification. Their assistance and an education loan saw me through!

Blessed music! The dorm matron for whom I worked had chosen me because of my music. Music not only got me to college, but it also brought wonderful people, rewarding avocation work, joyful experiences, and deeply satisfying avenues for volunteer service into my life."

- C Bierley - Alabama

. . .

"Grandmother Rushing was a member of Ephesus Primitive Baptist Church in Bulloch County, Georgia where services were held on the third Saturday and

Sunday. She would take us children, certainly, my cousin Julia, whom she raised, and me, to church. I don't remember any other cousin; though I am sure she took them all at one time or another.

Grandmother wanted us all exposed to that 'old time religion.' It seemed the preacher would never finish, and his voice would be so strong, and he would take his Bible and hold it up to make his point. My eyes were wide and I would be so still for a few minutes because I had never heard a preacher like this. After all, I was a Methodist and accustomed to a 'quiet' service with Sunday School and singing. It seemed pretty stern to a little girl. However, after a little while, my attention span was gone and I would wiggle. Grandmother always had a Brannen-Olliff Funeral Home fan which was pasteboard with a picture of Jesus on the front, or maybe a straw fan. I would squirm and wiggle. Then, she ever so gently would tap me on the leg with the fan or maybe she would fan my face a little. I thought the preacher would never finish, but finally the prayers and Amen were heard, and we were dismissed for 'Dinner on the ground.' I could hardly wait!

The children had to always wait for second table, and by the time I could fix my plate I knew just exactly what I wanted - some of all of it! The long tables were set up under oak trees on the side of the church, and the ladies were always so busy getting it all ready. They had covered the tables with white clothes, and oh, the food - chicken and dumplings, butter beans and dumplings, fried chicken, green beans, potato salad, deviled eggs. pork roast, ham, baked hens with dressing, fruit salads, white peas, and every kind of dessert. There were chocolate cakes, caramel cakes, jelly cakes, lemon pies, chocolate pies, banana pudding, and of course, the pound cake with white icing. The point cake was the best and still is my favorite!. My two aunts, Eddie Mae Donaldson and Sadie Brown still bake them and they are the best cakes in the world! Certainly in my world!

I was exposed early on to the best cooks in Bullock County, Georgia, and I know this is where my love of cooking began. There were big biscuits and corn bread and rolls and 'light' bread and iced tea which were jars - big gallon jars of sweetened iced tea. No one could come to 'Dinner on the Ground' without it! There were also great hunks of blocks of pure ice that went into your glass. The ice pick would chip it just to the right size.

I am sure this must have been summertime because it was hot. However, I remember it was cool under the trees and was peaceful, tranquil, and quiet. Only the sound of good friends, happy children playing, and folks enjoying good food and taking their Lord's Day for worship. These were farmers for the most part. There was no hunger. The families had worked hard, tilled their land, raised their food, and shared, and they were blessed.

By late afternoon, it was time to go. Grand mama gathered all their leftovers, her bowls, and jars, spoons, and knives. It was put back in her big old basket and covered with a much used dish towel. Then, we got in her two-door Chevrolet car and went back to Adabell, the farm. Two little girls had been exposed to lots of 'old-time religion', but remembering the dessert.

My brother, Dr. E. B. Rushing, after reading this story said to me, 'Elizabeth, this is a beautiful story, but you saw all of this through the eyes of a child. Don't you remember those were the Depression year and Daddy lost all of his money in the bank of Pascaqoula, Mississippi. That's why we had to move to Georgia.'"

- E Scott - Georgia

.   .   .

"Depression! Panic! Banks closing and people losing all their savings! Many committing suicide! How frightening these words sounded to a child such as I. The same awful words were heard on radio and from the lisp of grownups who spoke them with much shaking of heads and feverish gesturing and waving of their hands. But, the part that bothered me the most was the sad look on my parents' faces when they spoke the same words.

'How strange,' I thought. 'Why are Mama and Daddy so serious and sad? Why do they seem to be ignoring me instead of speaking happy words and smiling at me as they usually do?' Just then, they suddenly seemed to remember me. They then hugged me and explained what the evil sounding words meant. I felt better then. I thought, 'Oh, it is just about money matters. It isn't so bad as long as my parents are still smiling and happy. I don't mind having less money. Everything will be fine.'

A month before, we had moved into our brand new house. This house was the first one that was our very own. We had rented old houses before. My sister, Melba, and I thought the small bungalow was a palace. It was located twenty-six miles east of Charlotte, North Carolina, on a country hillside with dozens of dogwood trees which were now in full bloom. The place seemed to us to be an enchanted fairyland. So, for now it was easy for us to forget the bad news about a Depression.

As time went on I noticed that although our food was still delicious, we had meat only about once a week. Another thing I noticed that spring was that my parents planted a much larger garden than usual.

My sister and I liked working in the garden, but when the beans were beginning to blossom and the beetles were taking more than a fair sure, we were assigned a very, messy job. We had to pick off the beetles and crush them between two rocks. Of course, we hated this job, and after we had worked about an hour, Daddy passed by plowing. Melba called out to him, 'Daddy, how much are you paying us to do this hard work?'

He did not answer at first, but when he reached the end of the row, we heard him speak to our mule, 'Whoa, Beck.' As he took off his big straw hat and began fanning himself, he called us over to him.

41

'I'm sorry, girls,' he said, 'but there is very little money these days. Will you be sweet and just think how good these beans will be when the crop comes on and Mama cooks a big potful for dinner? But, if the beetles eat up the vines, there will be no beans.'

I though to myself he looked so tired and sad that it broke my heart. 'Sure, Daddy,' I said, 'after all beans are green like money and they are much better to eat!'

Mama, who was hoeing, had reached the end of the row. She came to join us in time to hear what I said. Then, she and Daddy both chuckled out loud. I remember how good that made me feel. So, as we continued to work, I had an idea.

'Melba,' I said, "let's put on a play tonight for Daddy and Mama. Maybe if it is funny, it will cheer them up and make them forget this terrible old Depression.'

Melba joyfully agreed... and give a funny play we did! Our parents laughed for the first time in a long while. After that, we worked on many other plays. We presented one almost every Friday night, and afterward, we usually played some board games. We enjoyed this because our parents always played with us. One of our favorites was Fox and Goose. We made our own board and used a red beans for the fox and yellow grains of corn for the geese.

On Sundays, we went to church, and after lunch, we enjoyed sitting on the porch to get some cool air and watch the few cars passing by.

I remember one particular Sunday. We heard a strange noise on the highway. It was the trotting of a horse. 'Look,' cried Daddy, 'there goes a Hoover cart!' We had heard that some people were making and using these because there was not much money for gas. Many blamed President Hoover for the Depression. That is why they named the carts after him. It was indeed a weird looking vehicle! It was just a board with a tongue to hitch the horse between. It had two wheels wearing automobile tires!

Melba and I ran down to the road and watched as long as it was in sight. We decided that riding in a Hoover cart would be more fun than anything else in the world. When we told our parents this, Daddy said, 'You'll probably have a chance to ride in one if this Depression does not end soon.'

As I recall, however, only one other Hoover cart appeared in our community. We never did have a chance to ride in one. People began pooling rides for essential trips to the grocery store. Often Daddy would catch up with his work and then he would walk to the store. It was four miles away, but he seemed to enjoy the trip.

We did not need to buy too many supplies because we grew our own food, and Mama canned the portion we did not eat fresh. We raised chickens so we had eggs and could kill a rooster now and then for our meat. We bought milk from a neighbor.

The thing I dreaded the most was that our school had to cut expenses. The first thing they did was to let our music teacher go. She had been teaching public school music and piano lessons. There was no other music teacher nearby, which meant no more piano lessons for Melba and me. This lasted for two years. We loved music so much that we practiced every free me moment we had, and because of this, we did not get too far behind.

The 'Great Depression' did not last forever even though it seemed a very long time. As I look back on that time, I feel thankful for it because we learned much from the experience. We learned to enjoy the simple things and to be thankful for the joy of just being alive. We learned to appreciate a beautiful sunrise or sunset and found that a drink of clear, fresh spring water tasted better and was more satisfying than a Coke.

- J Purvis - North Carolina

.   .   .

THE MIDWEST

"I had to start working as a paper boy during the depression. My father was ill lots of the time and would go from house to house asking for work.

We moved in with my grandparents. We lived in a two bedroom house and the family consisted of my grandparents, my parents, me and my sister. All of my paper route money I gave to my mother to help the family out. I needed five dollars for a bike. My grandmother loaned me the money, but she made sure that I repaid her out of my paper route money.

We ate anything to stay alive during the Depression. Our food was cooked over and over and we cooked everything we could.

My parents would go to the hog processing plant and get body parts people did not want. We got things like a hog's head or the feet. Mother would cook them and peel off the meat and make meat loaf out of it. My mother also boiled the chicken feet separately in order to get extra broth.

I hated Sundays because that was when my mother would fix 'lamb' for dinner. Instead, it was old mutton and it tasted like old piss to me. To this day, I do not like anything to do with sheep.

When my father was well, he would walk to the chicken hatchery on the outskirts of town. The people there would let him fill up a couple of baskets with rejected eggs. These were cracked or had not developed into an embryo. Our family ate the cracked eggs, and my father would clean up the whole eggs and sell them in the neighborhood.

We had a garden in the back of the house where we got our vegetables, and we had chickens roaming around the yard even though we lived in town. Neighbors chipped in and helped neighbors when things were bad.

During my teenage years, our summer entertainment was provided by the local night cop. When he made his rounds, we would throw rotten tomatoes at his car. He would cuss, get mad, and start to chase us. We always ran in different directions and he was so fat he never caught us.

I played lots of sports in school. I played baseball, football, and basketballs. My parents wanted me to get a job right after high school. They needed the money and were convinced they could get a a job at the railroad. I had different ideas and jumped at a athletic scholarship opportunity offered by a college.

When I was in college, I cleaned and was a handyman for the lady where I boarded. I washed her floors and windows, took care of the furnace, and did any other thing she asked me to do. I also kept the boiler running for a sorority house and did work for the math and chemistry professors. I also worked as a waiter in the dining room. I would steal any leftover food whenever I could.

When I got married, I did not own a suit. My grandfather had one that he had bought to be buried in. He let me borrow it to get married in. It was many years later when he died, but we buried him in that very same suit I got married in.

I swore to myself as I grew older that I would kill myself working at two, three, or four jobs before I would let my wife or kids work like I had to during the Depression. I have always been careful with my money. I know how hard it is to earn it.

- Iowa

.　　　.　　　.

"The crash came at a bad time for my parents. My mother had put all of her inheritance into a house, but mother and daddy were moving to another town. They had sold the house and put the money in the bank until they got settled in their new location. The banks crashed and Mother lost all of her money. She broke down and cried and cried and cried. Although they had houses later on in life, my mother never got over losing everything she had. (It was only $900, but it meant a lot to my mother.)

When I was twelve, I got a new pair of school shoes. They squeaked. I decided to soak them in water. My father came home and was very mad when he saw my new shoes soaking in water. He began chasing me around the table. I knew he was going to kill me so I ran as fast and hard as I could. We went round and round and round the table. My dad had a short fuse, but his anger was not long-lived. He began laughing and laughing. Then, I knew I was okay.

I recall our preachers comparing the NRA to be signs and omens of the Antichrist coming true as promised in the book of Revelations. (Note: National Recovery Administration. Destroyed by the Supreme Court in 1935.)

I also recall our social studies newspapers had many reports on life in Russia. I briefly thought Russian lives were better than ours because they shared everything.

My mother had a fear and distrust for American Indians. They had stolen from her family farm when she was a girl. Whenever we visited our cousins in South Dakota, Mother would made us cross the street if an Indian was walking down the same sidewalk we were on. She did not want us to be near them at all.

In 1936, I had scarlet fever. There were no antibiotics at this time and the doctor recommended I give blood. I was paid for my blood, and with this money of my own, I went out and bought some spiked heels. My father was very angry when he saw how I had spent my money. He said it was unnatural- that if God had wanted women to have spiked heels, he would have made them that way.

I was very popular in high school and had lots of boyfriends and girlfriends. One day, a boy stole one of my school papers. I had never noticed him until then. After college, I married him!

My best girlfriend and I went to see a fortuneteller one day. She told both of us we were going to have four children. We were very impressed by her and her predictions turned out right.

We were more fortunate than most. My father had a job with the utility company. He was never out of work. We never were hungry or did without and we had our cars.

I do remember us getting together baskets of food for those less fortunate than we were."

- Iowa

.　　　.　　　.

"My father was a plasterer and stuccoer and built some homes. He made it through the Great Depression better than most families did. I was only four years old at the time, and my brother was nine, we had a happy childhood.

My father was disgusted with the government and their "New Deals" which all failed to help resolve the depression. He always said, that if there had not been a war (World War II), the depression would have continued on and on, until our entire nation was bankrupted. He did not believe that the government could ever solve problems for the people. People have to solve their problems themselves.

If the people wasted as much as the government has always done, America would not be here today. Thomas Jefferson firmly stated, 'I am for a government rigorously frugal and simple.'"

- Iowa

.　　　.　　　.

"A flashback to the depression...

In 1929, I was seven years old. What is the most remembered happening of that time is what made the lasting effect. My father worked in Ohio. When the orders came in, he worked one or two days and maybe none at all. He could not afford to buy a license, gasoline, etc. He was concerned about the tires and put the car away in the garage. I can remember going down to watch the wheels being taken off and hung on the garage walls. The car was resting on concrete blocks until work came. I have no recollection of how long this lasted, but we could not get to church. It was too far to walk in the bad winter.

When spring came, our back yard was covered with wooden frames. Glass sash covered these and hot beds were the results. The first bottom layer was manure, then sand, and woods dirt mixed for seed planting. We grew cabbage and tomato plants and sold them for a few cents. With the garden and the plant money, we always had a well-nourished table, and some extras for our neighbors who did not fare as well.

We were happy and did not feel put on. We never had to ask for relief.

We now live in a retirement village and are still helping those less fortunate. May the joy continue!"

- Ohio

.　　　.　　　.

"My mother raised four children pretty much alone. We lived the simple life before the Depression. Our home was the center of our lives. We played cards a great deal for entertainment, mostly rummy or bridge.

I graduated from high school in 1932. Graduating seniors voted not to have caps and gowns. There were too many who could not afford them.

Dating had to be inexpensive. Movies were very cheap. I recall only one dinner-date at a restaurant. There was little "eating out."

My oldest sister graduated from Ohio State University and then taught until her marriage in 1929. My second sister became a nurse.

My brother, who was three years older, studied premed at Ohio State for three years beginning in 1929. He did not have enough money to finish which made him bitter for the rest of his life.

I did not take college preparatory courses in high school for I knew I would have to work. My secretarial skills served us well when my husband, a doctor, went into practice in 1938. After three years of general practice, he took a residency in orthopedics and left when he was called to duty in World War II.

My most vivid memory was the lack of security and my saddest moment was when a loved one died of rabies. We helped house two widows in addition to taking care of our own family. We pooled resources and endured the best we could. We only ate twice a day and my clothes we made over after they had been used by my older sister.

Our church was always a part of our lives. We attended often.

My husband and I were married in 1937 and have lived a happy life with our own three children."

- Ohio

.　　　.　　　.

"My most vivid memory of the Depression was that everyone was willing to do whatever job was available.

Grandpa was very much the leader of the family and everyone showed him a great deal of respect. We came from a large family and 30 family members would gather for dinner at someone's home. The turns were rotated.

Men and grown boys sat at the first serving, children at the second, and mother and the grown daughters ate at the third serving. My favorite meals were fried chicken, coconut cream pie, milk, iceberg lettuce with bacon. There was no worst meal for any of us.

I had one outfit for Sunday and five for school and play. Our gifts were mostly new clothes. We would seldom get an outgrown garment. I also received things like books, bicycles, candy, razors and cash.

My mother was a surgical nurse at a local hospital. When we needed surgery, Mother's former doctor did it. For other illnesses, the local doctor made us well. He made some of his own medicines and some contained paw-paws.

I was working in the State of Illinois Highway survey group when they were asked to help with the hiring for the PWA. The lines were long for these jobs that paid $3.95 for a 9 1/2 hour day. This was standard.

Mother taught school and was a saleslady in a local department store on Saturdays, holidays, and vacations. The children picked berries. Her daughter was a sales clerk at Silverblooms, also. I sold Saturday Evening Post, school books, and worked as a laborer on Pennsylvania Railroad construction, in a surveying crew, and in a brick yard.

There were times when people ("bums") came knocking on the door with a great deal of frequency asking for work or food. We always gave at least a sandwich. Sometimes, we also gave them a piece of cake or pie. The pride of the typical "Bum" caused him to insist on doing a small yard chore. He would leave with a "Thank you" and be on his way.

During these times, we never lost faith. Mother's energy and optimism left no room for a negative attitude."

- Illinois

. . .

"We were a close family of parents and four children. We were poor, but did not realize it.

Education was important. Each of us contributed in some way to income. My three brothers carried paper routes for years. One had his rib cage deformed by the heavy load on his left shoulder.

I worked in a soda fountain at the drugstore one summer, but in general, did my share working at home. I remember ironing shirts for my three brothers and father.

We all earned small scholarships and borrowed funds for tuition. My tuition at a teacher's college was $17.50 per quarter. We all lived at home while attending school. My brothers became engineers because there was a good engineering school in the city.

I remember men standing on street corners selling apples. My father instigated our sharing food and gifts of clothing with families in the neighborhood at Christmas when he knew they needed those things. Our own gifts were practical ones, such as clothing, with an occasional toy. We had what we needed - an outfit each season. We always had a large garden.

My wedding to a fellow teacher was a simple one in my home, with only the family and a couple of close friends present.

My mother's uncle, a widower, stands out in my memory for his varied contributions over the years. These contributions consisted of used bicycles to a couple of gold coins at graduation time. I am sure he helped out my mother in ways I never knew about, and I still remember him when I look at items of a walnut picture frame and glass bowls from his home following his death.

My saddest memory was of the death of my oldest brother. He was killed in a car accident by a boy in an old truck who did not make it around a curve and ran into my brother's car. He was on his way to another city to a good job waiting for him."

- Central Indiana

.　　　.　　　.

"We kept moving a lot during the Depression. As a result, I did not have any friends. I was born in Michigan and remember living in Nebraska, Kansas, and Ohio.

Before the Depression, my father had a job at Dupont. He left it for what he felt was a better job with a smaller outfit. He lost his job when the Depression came.

My uncle had a furniture and hardware store in Ohio. He set my father up with a hardware store in another town, Middleport, Ohio. However, the hardware store flooded, and he was out of business and a job again.

Mother did not like Middleport. She felt trapped there.

I had two brothers and no sister. My cousin, Jean, was like a sister to me. She was three years older and was raised by my grandmother when her own mother died of pneumonia. Jean made me my first bra.

My grandmother would say anything that came to her mind. She called boys "Pee-crookeds." and girls "Split-Tails." She liked to shock people and nobody slept or got bored when Grandma was around. I remember being terribly embarrassed by her when I had a date to go roller skating. The boy was late, and when he did arrive, she told him she thought he was not going to come.

When I graduated form high school, I wanted to be a writer, but my parents could not afford it. I went to a local nurses school. My brothers did go onto college and one became a doctor.

My mother died of uterine cancer when I was 18. I remember her walking through the house and blood clots would fall on the floor. She had cobalt treatments and this destroyed her kidneys. So, the cancer did not really kill her.

I came home from school to help my father and brothers out. When I was in school, I had a friend who had trouble waking up to the alarm clock. She would leave notes in the bathroom asking someone to wake her up at 6:15. I was working split shifts at the hospital and taking my classes in the afternoon. There were many times, I would come in at midnight and knock on her door.

"It's 6:15," I would say and then I would run to my room and close the door. Of course, she would get up and wander the hall trying to find out who was pulling tricks on her.

Because I came in late at night, many of the girls would ask me to bring in food after work. There was one time I fixed a rat sandwich for one girl. She started to eat it, but stopped when the tail fell out.

When I started nursing, there were no orderlies or nurses aides in hospitals. We had to do everything ourselves from emptying bedpans to giving enemas.

I did not have much money. I remember when I entered a restroom with pay toilets, I would crawl under the stalls rather than pay."

- MLM - Ohio

.   .   .

"This is a combination of my memory of the Depression as well as the way it affected my family. I was born on a farm in 1913. My family consisted of ten children in the area of Cousins. I was the seventh child in our family.

Our parents were very anxious for all of the children to get the best possible education. Four of the children, older than me, graduated from the Teacher College. We lived in Davies County, Kentucky. Our farm was located in a rich farming area.

I was a sophomore in high school when the real damage of the Depression struck our family. It especially affected myself and my younger brothers and sisters.

The prices for agriculture products and land value became very low. Because of this, my father lost the farm to a bank that foreclosed on a note my father had signed. Corn was selling for ten cents a bushel. Hogs sold for three cents per pound, and hay could not be baled for the price that was being paid.

All my father knew was farming. So, he worked out an agreement with the bank to take over an old farm located 30 miles from where we lived. This farm was subject to flooding from the Ohio and Green rivers. This move took us away from a nice farm to a poor farm and away from our friends and kin folks.

Four of my cousins whose parents had died came to live with us. On this new place, we traveled by boat sometimes in order to get to it.

I had to go to a new high school where I did not know anyone. When I missed the bus, I had to walk six miles or I would stop at a brother's house in the town. He was out of work and was trying to get along on just a few days of work.

Our family would furnish my brother, his wife, and his four children with chickens and pork, and in the summer with vegetables from our garden. My mother canned many of our vegetables and would share these with my brother's family. When I found out I had to stop at my brother's home, we would eat oatmeal with evaporated milk. (I still don't like oatmeal.)

During high school, I became involved in Vocational Education in agriculture classes. I was active in the Future Farmers of American organization. I became the State Treasurer and all the funds were sent to me and the dues from each chapter. All of these funds were deposited in the Central Trust Bank in Owensboro, Kentucky. When the bank holiday was declared by the President, we lost our funds and we never received more than ten percent of the money back.

After graduation from high school, we had no money for me to go on to college. I spent the next year working on the farm.

In 1932, my father took me to Bowling Green, Kentucky where my older brothers and sisters had gone to school. He arranged for me to stay in the Pavilion where the dairy cows were kept and I milked the cows to pay for my room. He also arranged for me to work waiting on tables at a boarding house for my meals. When I enrolled, I signed up for R.O.T.C. and that furnished my uniforms.

After one year of college, I received a temporary teaching certificate and obtained a job teaching in a one-room school in my home community. School was only for seven months and then I would go back to college for the spring and summer sessions. Again, I milked cows and waited tables and I did this for three years.

Then, I got a job working in the college kitchen. This job furnished a room and meals. The lady that was the head of the food service was not only a food serving person, but she was very much concerned with the welfare of the students who worked for her. It was here that I met my future wife.

In 1937, the levee along the Ohio River broke and the water got over the farm where my mother and father lived. They lost all of the livestock and there was a great deal of damage to the farm. The Red Cross came in to help bury the dead livestock and provided some clothing. My father became sick after this happened and never really recovered.

Among the happier times I remember was when I got the job working in the college kitchen. It enabled me to continue my schooling and I graduated with a B.S. in Agriculture in 1938.

My family was a close-knit group. I had 80 first cousins on my mother's and father's side. We held many picnics in the local parks. We wore largely home-made clothes and ate largely the farm products we grew.

We had very few gifts and these were usually homemade. What little money we had came from the sale of products such as butter, eggs, chickens, and hogs. In addition to taking care of our family, we also helped two black families make it through the years.

I met my wife while I was in college and she also worked in the dining hall at the college and taught in a one-room school. She taught high school a year after graduation and we married in 1939.

Our marriage was at the home of her parents and our flowers came from the family farm fields. Our wedding was very plain, and we had country ham and a big cake for our wedding meal. We got married on a Sunday morning and everyone had breakfast afterwards. The minister had to go several miles to church where he was to preach that day. We had a few friends and her family as guests.

None of my family was ever arrested for any crime. When anyone in the family got sick, the family did the best they could to doctor us. We used home medicines and remedies.

My worst meal was oatmeal with evaporated milk. My favorite meals was, and still is, fried chicken and coconut pie.

We never had more than two sets of clothes. One set was for Sunday and the other were work clothes. Hand-me-downs were mostly from the older members of the family. We never lost faith.

My wife and I had two children. Our daughter has her ED. degree in education. Our son joined the military following his graduation from college. He later obtained three MA degrees. He died in 1989 with brain cancer. We have four Grandchildren and one Great Grandchild.

So many things my wife and I do reminds us that we are from the Depression period. We never waste anything. Our investments and our lifestyle is very conservative. I retired after working in the food industry for 35 years and then taught for ten years at Arizona State University. We are survivors."

- RGL - Kentucky

.   .   .

"I was born in a small town in Iowa and lived there until I graduated from high school in 1927. I attended college and worked in various towns in Iowa until World War II came along in 1941.

The Depression that started in 1929 for the rest of the country hardly made any difference to our family. We had always had depression. We learned at an early age that we must work hard and spend no money unless we had to. I remember believing that we were happier than most families even if they had more money to spend.

I worked my way through college and law school at a total cost of $1400 above what I could earn. The worst year was 1931- not just for what happened to me, but to my whole family. I worked all summer on a paving crew. It was back-breaking work at 40 cents an hour. I saved up $200. I paid $90 tuition at college and had $110 to finish the school year. Then, the bank went broke and I lost it all.

Even worse, my mother had saved $1000 in a lifetime of hard work and it all went too. Then, my father's business went broke and he had no employment at the age of 62. To make all things worse, my mother nearly died from a operation and never did regain her normal good health. But, we all survived. I wonder if young people of modern times have any conception of the hard times of those days?

The happiest day of all times was my wedding day on June 18, 1939. We had waited a long time through two years of teaching, three years of law school and one more year of paying debts, but finally the great day arrived. We were married in a church with flower decorations, a Best Man, and Matron of Honor, and I still think it was beautiful. My wife made her own bridal gown at a total cost of $7.00.

We lived a quiet life of hard work, inexpensive vacations and practical gifts if we could afford any. We paid cash for everything and never incurred any debts or owed any bills.

My wife was a fine cook, and I can't remember any food that I did not like. My favorite was fried chicken.

The hard times gradually got a little better. We were gradually feeling a little more prosperous when World War II came in 1941."

- LHG - Iowa

.   .   .

"During the Depression, I was young enough at the time that I never felt bothered by what was going on. My memories are that we always had food on the table. Dad always had a huge garden and there were fruit trees and bushes for jams and jellies.

My older sister, Isabel, always made our holidays and birthdays delightful. She was eleven years older than me and the house was always decorated. Since my birthday is on July 4, she sometimes had to chase me around the house to put on my Fourth-of-July dress she had made with stars and stripes. She dressed a fat cousin of mine as a fairy and made a bee outfit for my brother. Then, we would put on a play for the adults. There was one time we had to have a few minutes to change the scenery. By the time, we were through, the adults had left and gone for a ride!

Mother did lots of sewing and would make over different clothes so that we were always clean and neat. I will always cherish the memory of my mother reading the Bible every evening after the house had quieted. She was a strong person, and I was fortunate she was my mother.

When we became sick, it was cod liver oil. Ugh! It was always put in orange juice. That almost ruined orange juice for me.

We did not have much money but I never knew we were poor. An uncle would sometimes help out, but I did not learn that until much, much later.

My three older siblings had jobs as dad had lost his. Then, my sister Catherine got tuberculosis and Dick married so that left my sister Isabelle with quite a load on her shoulders. I am sure it was a struggle for the older ones, but we managed.

There were hoboes who stopped by the house and we always gave them something to eat. Food was probably the only thing we bought and that was always with cash. Life was so simple then we did not need much and my memories are that we had what we needed."

- BWG - Iowa

. . .

"My memories of the Depression years are conditioned by the urban setting in which I lived, the well-educated home with which I was blessed, and the fine school systems in our city. Our home life was centered in the life of a very active church where both my parents were leaders in supportive roles.

Youth work was a way of life for my brother, who was four years older than I, and for me. Therefore our social life was not diminished by lack of ready cash. For instance, youth choir of some 75 assorted voices meant smaller sing-along groups before, after, and in-between other activities!

I had skipped the equivalent of two full grades in the course of grade school and this placed me with friends usually two years older than I. To this day, my husband loves hearing me recount 'my most embarrassing moment.' At the end of my freshman year in high school, sitting across the aisle from my 'heart throb', who was a handsome junior with a beautiful tenor voice, a long-time girl friend suddenly turned before class bell to wish me a Happy Birthday. Mr. Handsome joined the good wishes, but ruined my day when he asked my age. My meek reply of 'thirteen' brought forth the withering 'Do you mean you have only been <u>twelve</u> all this year?' So much for maturity!

I was scarcely aware of the shortage of funds that was reality to many of my classmates. Our school system placed great emphasis on music in all aspects. It owned many of the more expensive instruments and provided us all with private lessons on the ones we owned or borrowed from the school.

Looking back, I realize that one of the outstanding French horn players used a school instrument, was taught entirely by school instructors, and at the end of high school was offered a chair in the then prestigious Kryl's Band in Washington, D.C. The school owned harps, Sousaphones, and other such fine instruments which no students could have dreamed of affording. No wonder our concert band achieved first place in Class A in the state and ranked in the top six nationally which meant we joined our 'talents' under the direction of John Phillip Sousa which was a lifetime thrill for this then 12 year old!

My parents had met during their freshman year on a college campus and remained true lovers from that day throughout their extended years of courtship and nearly 55 years of married life. They lost all their worldly goods more than once so the Depression years were not a new challenge to them.

Some years before the Depression hit, my father had gone into the hardware business where his electrical engineering degree stood him in good stead with the increasing importance of radio sales as well as other major appliances. He had carried his customers' credit on his own in those earlier years. However, increasingly he became the loser as jobs were lost, payments were not made, and he had to repossess unpaid for merchandise too often for his sympathetic nature to endure.

More than once some of us family remembers would be out in the car or store truck when he entered an angry household to retrieve what had not been paid for. It broke his heart to put on a tough exterior when he felt so sorry for the family concerned! Of course, the only answer was to join one of the large commercial credit companies and let them handle future credit accounts. More families enjoyed nearly normal Christmas celebrations with written-off credit accounts, as well as other seasons's extended credit for the clean-up, fix-up hardware than out-of-work men had time on their hands to do. The only trouble with his open-heart policy was that wholesalers from whom he purchased expected prompt payment. That conflict caused many tight squeezes on the home front and allowed NO surplus cash for a daughter who wanted to enter college!

Since I graduated from high school just after my sixteenth birthday, it seemed like a good idea to enroll in a local business college where I could learn skills that my college-bent courses and over-filled extracurricular hours of choral and band had never allowed time for in high school. Enrollment was at an all-time low and the instruction was guided toward personal preferences and needs.

I chose a little known, but quickly learned system of shorthand which enabled me to be taking shorthand accurately in three months. Typing, bookkeeping, comptometry and other then offered courses proved to be a breeze. To save bus money, I often walked the more than two miles and used the cash for my lunch at the counter in Kresge's where it totaled 15 cents.

Business college came to an abrupt end when one afternoon the owner came into the room where I was working, sat on my desk and announced that he did not have the heart to accept another month's tuition from me, adding that I had learned all I had come for, and he hadn't had an inquiry for even an experienced secretary in months, let alone an inexperienced 16 year old. However, I have been eternally grateful to him because his training did prepare me for serving as secretary to the librarian in the seminary where my husband and I spent the first two wonderful years of our marriage! The shorthand and typing proved priceless when I did finally get to college and in many areas since.

Another Depression picture in my mind is the constant knock on the back door where hungry men asked for something to eat. My mother never turned anyone away without at least a sandwich, even though she was well aware of the marking on our garage on the alley side telling all 'tramps' that here was a sure-bet for being served.

Now, the front door sales parade offered a little more resistance on her part. She was a 'soft touch' to purchase at least a little something from the Fuller Brush man or one selling vanilla, etc., but the promoters of horseradish roots heard quickly that no one in this household ate that stuff! (I did not know until college years that I actually liked it in mild amounts!).

And, woe to those in the constant stream of those who wanted to sell chances on anything! Her staunch stand in opposition to any form of gambling, large or small, always brought a statement to that effect along with her refusal to purchase. Her reasoning was that it might be the only time that child or man might ever hear opposition to gambling, so she made her witness. I should add that her witness, as well as my father's on the same subject, carried over to me to this day. Not many months ago when I tried to be gentle in my refusal to participate in a small 'buy a chance' event for the umpteenth time, the seller remarked 'Oh, I get it. I just learned you are a clergy wife.' I quickly assured her that was not the reason, but that it was a life-long belief.

When asked what some of us teenagers did in the years between high school and college when jobs were non-existent, I am grateful again for the wonderful family relationships I enjoyed. There were rich with mother-daughter sharing of cooking, sewing, shopping, and special events contrived out of seemingly nothing.

A group of some five or six of us girls agreed to each make a quilt. We met together once a week for sewing together and sharing the week's progress. By nature, I dislike unfinished projects, so I completed mine with an intricate design of sixty pieces in each block. My mother had agreed to pay for the quilting to be done by a skilled quilter (our church custodian's wife) who gladly accepted all the quilts she could get for a penny a yard of thread used - an unheard of bargain by today's prices!

I have understood the other girls completed their quilts at various stages of their lives. My sister-in-law's granddaughter completed hers not too many years ago. Actually, that is an advantage, since we gave ours hard use the first thirty years of our married lives and finally discarded it.

Our wedding fell during later Depression years when most folks had adjusted to frugal living pretty well. We invited just 65 guests for our church wedding, carefully avoiding any 'open church' announcement to keep refreshment costs manageable. A neighbor and church friend, familiar with church serving, was willing to mix and serve our fruit punch with the lovely wedding cake we personally took care of.

I made my own wedding dress of white taffeta, trimmed with velvet, and the veil's headpiece was decorated with the pearl ornament from my mother's wedding dress. The cost of the dress was $5.35 and the veil plus crescent head piece brought the total to nearly ten dollars. White satin sandals at $3.95 were my extravagance.

That Depression wedding took and it is still going strong 57 years later! Neither of us has any regrets. We only have gratitude for the strong basics we received for life."

- WS - Indiana

.   .   .

"I was born in Louisville, Kentucky on February 13, 1915, but lived most of my life in Indiana. My father was a minister who never had a good salary. My mother had been an orphan and was raised in a home that treated her well, but worked her pretty hard, I feel. She married and had a son, my only brother. Her husband died and she met my father and they were married for 40 years.

My brothers was ten years older than I. Sadly, he had polio which left him somewhat impaired in walking so he had to drop out of high school, but later got to a business school.

My father never stayed long in any church, though he was a good man, and we were on marginal income <u>at all times.</u> When the Depression hit, his church nearly folded and we moved to Indianapolis, Indiana where we hoped to find some income of any kind.

My only uncle lived there. He had a good job, but helped us little. Dad got up a case of sewing helps and went door-to-door to try to sell them. I got a newspaper route and there were <u>many</u> times when the only money coming into the house was from my route.

Our house was a duplex and at one point when we might have been evicted, the owner let us stay for months without pay. He said it protected his property from 'having the siding pulled off for fire wood or being used by vagrants.'

I was in a large high school of 6,000 students and took precollege courses. I was also in a super church that had a large youth group and thoughtful preaching and programs. The church had a gym and church teams played there. I got 25-50 cents a night (two nights a week) that helped us. We also started a food stand near a tire factory miles from our home. My mother fixed things for us to carry over there and sell. I learned to paint houses and painted three in our neighborhood for 10-15 cents an hour.

Things got a little better for us when my brother wrote a letter to his fellow polio victim - FDR. As a result, he got to be a timekeeper on a W.P.A. project and later got a job at the Marion County Court House.

I entered a state oratorical contest which had a first prize of a one year scholarship to Frank College in Franklin, Indiana. I lost out in the regional the first year that I tried, but won the second year. I wanted to be a lawyer, but the influence of two professors, and a more open approach to Christian thought and faith led me to the ministry, for which I am forever grateful!

In college, I started to date a girl who had also been in the contest. We fell in love and were married at the beginning of my second year of seminary. (I failed to note that we graduated with honors after doing independent work in our senior year).

My parents-in-law were just the greatest! They were both college graduates. He owned a fine hardware and electric store.

A couple in our first church had something of my kind of experience during the Depression. That is, he had. One evening we counted up how many "Depression time" and high school, college, and grad school jobs we had done. I had 27!

Because we were able to get reasonably good salaries, we became the major support of my parents after my brother died. When my father died, my mother came to live with us for 13 years.

We have had a good life, with two fine sons and their wives and four granddaughters. We had splendid churches. We have been strict budgeters (my wife has helped many couples with money problems), and we now live in a life care community in Tempe, Arizona in a two bedroom, two bath cottage. We both have had our 80th birthdays this year!"

- RS - Indiana

.   .   .

"I was eleven years old when the Depression came. Our family lived in a small town of 1500 people in the state of Iowa. My father was going to medical school training to be a General Practitioner.

My most vivid memory was that before the Depression came my older brother was paid $2.50 an hour to help clean up my father's office. It was my turn after the Depression started and I only earned 25 cents an hour!

I also remember people wearing $29 silk shirts before the Depression. Afterwards, they bought shirts that cost $2.50.

There was no money during the Depression and my father was paid with food for his services. People brought us Sunday dinners, dairy products, and butchered meats.

There were three levels of mush in our house - water mush, milk mush, and cream mush. Times were bad when we got water mush and times were good when we had cream mush. Water mush was real bad and is my least favorite meal.

My grandmother was Norwegian and did not speak English. She died in my freshman year in high school, but I do not recall much about the funeral.

My mother loved to bake and was a real good cook, but my dad did all of the shopping. Mother also remade suits for my brothers from my father's clothes and she knitted all of our socks. Shoes were well-worn hand-me-downs.

My mother fed every hobo who came by. Most of the hoboes were older men in their 40's and 50's. One time a hobo came by the house and mother was not home. I did not give him anything to eat and he told me he hoped I was old and hungry one day.

For games, we skated and sledded in the winter. We also had iron hoops which were about one foot in diameter. These came from wagons. We would roll our hoops with a stick all over town. We had a great time.

We also played marbles. We had aggies, tommies, glassies, and steelies. Steelies were ball bearings.

If a boy who had the ball was called home, our game would stop. Then, we would form gangs and wrestle each other or play King of the Hill.

A small glass of fountain soda cost five cents and a big candy bar (bigger than the 50 cent bars of today) cost five cents, too. Breakfast was 15 cents and a good lunch or dinner cost 35 cents. You could eat very well on a dollar a day.

In 1936, I hitchhiked to Illinois to get a job at a Del Monte canning factory. I rode in a rumble seat with two men. Their car had no windshield and it rained on us. When we got to where I was going, I told them I didn't have much money to repay them for the ride. I took them to a diner and got them two hot dogs and a cup of coffee for 15 cents. A rented room cost $7.00 a month.

At Christmas time, we received one present. It was either a book or a toy. I usually got a book.

Our cousins would visit on July Fourth. We would have a good time shooting off firecrackers until five o'clock in the morning. I am sure we bothered all the neighbors with our noise and racket. The people who owned the fireworks store would also give the town a fireworks display of fireworks which had not been sold for the celebrations.

I began college in 1936. I worked in a canning factory and as a janitor for a bank. My father paid my room rent.

One of the things I remember Roosevelt doing was setting quotas up for the farmers. He did this in order to get rid of any surplus and to buoy up farm prices. If a farmer had too many hogs or too much corn planted, he had to destroy them by killing the animals or plowing under the corn. My uncle was a farmer and found out he had five hogs too many. A family member suggested he give the hogs away, but the law said they were to be destroyed. So, my uncle killed those five hogs and buried them."

- EMO - Iowa

. . .

"My most vivid memory of the Depression was of putting cardboard in my shoes when they had worn out. I also recall brushing my teeth with Ivory Soap.

Our family had twin brothers born in 1933. I recalled feeling as if I was a "hired hand." I lived in a small apartment with my parents and four of us children. It was located in Beverly Hills, a beautiful suburb in southwest Chicago.

Christmas and Easter were happy holidays. My saddest moment was when my grandparents passed on.

My father worked for the P.R.R. in Chicago. I recall happy summer holidays were spent on my grandmother's farm in the Poco's Mountains of Pennsylvania. We had passes on the railroad so that we could get there.

I recall traveling alone to Philadelphia, Pennsylvania at school holidays and sightseeing. Also on school holidays, my father would take me to new railroad stations over night. I had to study up on the cities and guide my father around the city. This put me in good stead for married life later.

In 1948, I went overseas to Antwerp, Belgium with a ten-month old daughter. We lived there for seven years and then for 25 years outside London, England. My husband worked for Swift and Company in the export department and we traveled home on ocean liners every three years. Because we have many British pensions, our income is reduced and we have lost $5,400 of our income.

My Depression years and building up Europe after World War II have put me in good stead for living on a reduced income. I left my heart in Europe and would leave the United States tomorrow if I could. (We live in a retirement community now as my husband has Alzheimers.)

I dislike the "materialistic society" we live in now.

I recall a good youth in my depression years at my church and in Girl Scouts."
- Illinois

. . .

"Our family lived in Louisville during the Depression. I recall we had a country doctor. My happiest holiday was Christmas and I received dolls.

My favorite meals during the Depression was corn bread and milk. My worst meal was when we ate hog meat. I also recall going to the store for candy as a special treat. I had two or three outfits to wear.

Roosevelt was a fine man. He saved us all with the W.P.A. work."
- Kentucky

. . .

"I grew up in Jasper, Michigan. It was a very small town outside of Adrian. The town had a post office, store, and grain elevator.

I recall I had a very stable life. I was nine years old when the Depression began.

My father was a mechanic. He had his own garage. He later sold this business and began working for City Service Oil Company. He traveled the state working as a power prover. A power prover measured the efficiency of combustion engines.

My mother was a homemaker. She was a perfectionist when it came to the house. I recall helping her with ironing, washing, and dusting. We would start cleaning each morning and finish by noon. Then, we would clean up after lunch. Our afternoons were free for visiting and socializing.

I had one close girlfriend and our time together was very structured. We would only be allowed to play together at one house for 30 minutes. Then, we would go to the other's house and play for exactly another 30 minutes.

We played croquet or went on long walks with little umbrellas over our head. I recall only one vacation. We went on a camping trip to Wisconsin when I was nine. My girlfriend's family had a summer cottage on a lake 20 miles from our town. It was always a great treat for me to be invited to join her family for a week.

Our family was scattered and I do not remember many visits or big family get-togethers. Our holidays were usually spent alone with only our family of four. I remember one Christmas when we did not even have a tree.

I had no bicycle. Instead, I used roller skates to get around. My happiest present was when I received my class ring. I was delighted, surprised, and very pleased because I thought we could not afford it. It was a wonderful gift.

I recall my mother loved greens and I did not like them. Our meals were plain and we ate lots of chicken. A special treat was hot biscuits with maple syrup for dinner. There were many times when my father was paid with goods and food. I recall we always had lots of syrup.

My mother loved to cook for company and big crowds. A big bag of groceries cost $2.00. We got many of our vegetables and meats from relatives who lived on farms. We canned vegetables such as corn and beans.

I had an aunt who had eight children. We went to her farm and helped her can in the summer because it took a lot to feed all of them. She was a very good seamstress and sewed many of my clothes as my mother did not sew. I had one church dress.

I remember a few times when we took the train to my aunt's farm. It was fun and exciting.

Crime such as robbery or petty thievery was non-existent in our community. The doors were never locked. If you did lock your door, anyone else could get in because all the doors used the same skeleton key. Each summer, the gypsies would come through our town. It was the only time we locked our doors when they visited.

The only crime I recall was when we had a fire at the granary. It was a tremendous fire and was later determined to be arson.

In high school, I sang in the chorus, worked on the school newspaper and annual, and was a member of the debate club. I graduated in 1937.

My mother did not drive. When I grew older, I spent much of my time driving her to where she needed to go.

I had a summer job in the Soil Conservation Office. Farm prices were very low during the Depression. The office was started to pay farmers to idle their land. I did maps on the farms in the area. My father thought idling the land was a terrible thing to do.

In 1937, I went to college as a day student. I trained to be a teacher at Adrian College, a Methodist school. My tuition was $100 a semester. This sum was beyond the affordability of many of my friends. During college, I worked for a while as an assistant to the French professor. I graded papers, ran errands, and even dusted her apartment!

There was a hamburger stand not far from the campus. Hamburgers cost 15 cents.

Saturdays were big days for our town. That was when the farmers came to town with all of their children. Stores would stay open until 9:30 p.m. There were free movies, drawings on Bank night where they gave away used cars, and the grocery store and a drawing once a week for free groceries, too.

My vividest memory was that many people took their lives in our county when the Depression came."

- OH - Michigan

.   .   .

"Although this happened before the Depression, my father died when I was 15 months old. My mother was left with three children to raise, no income, and no insurance.

My sister was 10 years older than me and my brother was 12 years older. My mother began to sell baked goods. My brother and sister helped her sell them. She was then offered a job at a YWCA cafeteria and became the manager. With her job as manager, it provided me with the right to eat at the cafeteria. I was given 18 cents for a meal.

The cafeteria folded and my sister was now working as a teacher in Holland, Michigan. We moved there and my mother rented a large house and ran it as a boarding house. It later became part of a fraternity house for the Knickerbockers.

I recall we did not have much cash. We did have a radio and I had many favorite programs. I enjoyed Jack Armstrong, the All-American Boy, Little Orphan Annie, and on Sunday, listened to foreign legion programs.

We also put together many jigsaw puzzles. The bigger and more complicated it was only made it better. Sometimes we would work on a puzzle for a month. When we finished, we would swap our puzzles around with other people. We also had friends with cars and would have picnics on a nearby lake. My mother always took Spanish Rice.

In 1931, my sister did a terrible thing. She got married on us! During this time, my grandparents' house burned down. Grandfather never got over this. He took to the bed, had a stroke, and died.

The house was rebuilt and we moved to Pal Myra, in southern Michigan. It was a town of 200 people and everybody knew everything about each other. I joined my mother and grandmother there.

My father's father was a farmer and Presbyterian minister. He died during this time and left his daughter, who had devoted her life to him, alone. I moved to the farm with this aunt.

The farm was 240 acres and had animals and grew crops. The farm also grew ginseng which was a root used in medicines. I was very unhappy on the farm and had a very tough time. I did not get to see my mother often and missed her. This was in 1933 and I was a junior in high school. I recall my aunt gave me 20 cents to buy lunch. It was the only cash I ever saw.

In high school, I played football and in the band. I was a clarinet player. I did not have a bicycle and I got around on roller skates when I wanted to travel.

At Christmas, I received one toy. I recall I got an electric train that ran on big batteries. We had lots of snow in Michigan and I also had a sled and skis.

I graduated from high school in 1935 in Adrian, Michigan. I had no money to go on to college so I worked for two years at a hardware store. The building was owned by my grandmother.

My grandmother died and my mother and I lived on in their house. The store rent was our only income. I recall we took the rent in groceries instead of money. I also got a Model A Ford and met my future wife during this time.

My wife's father encouraged me to throw my hat into their house one day. He said if it did not get thrown back out I might have a chance with his daughter. The hat stayed in the house and we began to see each other. I did not have any money and the things we did together were not fancy or expensive.

I recall my grandmother had a cat she doted on when she was alive. She pampered that cat and would go to the store and buy it liver. I thought that was odd because we could hardly afford to feed ourselves, much less a cat!

I went to school at TMI in 1937. We had no guidance counselors to help us decide what courses we should take. I took a concentrated business degree. I ran out of money during my first year. During my next year, the school financed a

63

loan for me and provided me with a band scholarship. I also waited tables in order to finish my education. During the summer, I baled straw and recall it was hard, backbreaking work. A friend and I also developed a very profitable business scheme by selling deserts to other students.

In 1939, I was employed by Eastman Kodak and moved to Kingsport, Tennessee. It was a large town of 25,000 people. I thought it was a really big city even though the cows still were pastured right in the middle of the town.

I began work as a Buyer and was paid $20 a week. I paid $1.00 a day for a room at a boarding house and this dollar also included three meals. This left me with $13 to buy clothes and pay off my school debt.

Movies were 25 cents. Candy bars were 15 cents.

An Arrow shirt was $2.00. Dress shoes were $5.00.

A suit with vest and pants cost $22.50, and a necktie was also thrown in when you bought a shirt!"

- ELH - Michigan

.   .   .

"1930 was a beautiful year for me. My husband and I drove to Waukegan, Illinois and got married. He was 25 and I was 24. What a beautiful day. He was a Marine still in service. My home was Chicago, We danced all night with friends.

My sister was going to New York City to be a model. She lived there eleven years. I enjoyed going to visit her. We had wonderful times while my husband was in the service. He has been around the world three times, at Iwo Jima during the war with the boys at the time the fellows raised the Flag. He was away for two years.

Meanwhile, I was employed at Marshall Field in Chicago. The glorious store on State Street that closed the curtains every Sunday for respect. I earned the huge amount of $16 a week and was employed in the foundation department. I was later sent to Oak Park, Illinois and employed at Fields for eleven years.

I recall some ladies had their children born in the Store draped behind the curtains. I also remember older employees outlived their time and were discharged when they were 70 years old. They usually jumped from the ninth floor down the stairway. It was pitiful.

My mother was a good seamstress. She made all our clothes even to go dancing. She had 2 1/2 yards of beautiful material and she made us dressed to wear while dancing. She made them so well we would come home with the dresses and in fine shape. Our dancing dressed had a workout!

Mother had made sure all four of us were good dancers. The girls would stand in line in order to dance with my brother.

My favorite meals is still Chop Suey.

I have sewn all my life. Mother was a marvelous teacher. She never took all four of us shopping. Instead, she took our measurements and brought the clothes home. We were always well dressed.

We were Catholic, but I married a Swede. He, like most men, does not go to church, but I still do.

We have lived in several states. Our last move to to the Eastern Star Masonic home. My husband is in the nursing home at age 91 and I am also there at age 89. It has been a beautiful life just being together. You must have a beautiful life too. Enjoy it."

- CBA - Illinois

.   .   .

"I was twelve years old when the Depression started. Our family was very poor. We darned socks and patched our hose. When all of the girls would go to the store for a coke, I would not go with them because I did not have the five cents the coke cost. I never asked my parents for money because I knew it was not there.

We lived with my grandparents. Our kitchen was in the basement. I recall my mother sticking her hand in the oven to test the heat when she baked. She always knew when it was just the right temperature. My favorite was when she baked a sunshine cake. It was a golden color and had a texture like angel food cake.

I always went home for lunch when I was in school. We did not have a lot of clothes, but we always made sure they were clean.

After dinner, it was my brother's and my responsibility to clean the dishes. I was slow and sometimes my brother would chase me around the table with a butcher knife. He was always in a hurry because he and a ball game to go to when dinner was finished.

We had a chicken house in the back. A chicken had to weigh four pounds before my grandfather would kill it. I recall many times when my grandmother would call out, 'Charlie, go out and kill a chicken.'

Our entertainment was Sunday school and church. In the late 1930's, my future husband would get up early and milk the cows on Sunday morning. Then, he would pick me up at 7:00 A.M. We would drive to the dairy and delivery the milk. Then, Speck, would swipe some chocolate milk and we would drive around drinking our milk. Afterwards, he would drop me off at home so that I could go to Sunday school.

I remember I also used to go the Creamery and watch them making butter. Every once in a while, some of the men would put some butter on paper and give it to me. I would sit there and eat it. I loved butter. Sometimes, when my mother wasn't looking, I would snitch it from the table."

- VP - Iowa

.   .   .

"The Depression was really tough going for me and my family. My parents had a farm. We almost lost it. We dressed chickens and picked and sold plums. We burned corn instead of coal for heat."
- Iowa

.   .   .

"I was born and raised outside a small town in northern Indiana. My father owned a dairy farm. My father and his two brothers had the contract to supply The Culver Military Academy with all its milk requirements. This helped our family weather the storm of the Depression years quite well.

Of course, my mother always had a huge vegetable garden, fruit tress and bushes, and lots of chickens. No one ever went hungry on the farm.

To me, the Depression was something happening far away. Food was never a problem and hand-me-downs were considered most suitable then for clothing."
- LR - Indiana

.   .   .

"I was in first grade when the banks closed. We were in our reading class after lunch. Our little chairs were arranged in a half circle, with the teacher sitting facing us. Another teacher came into the room and whispered something in her ear. They both had incredulous looks on both their faces. They hugged each other, burst into tears, grabbed their coats, and dashed out of the room.

We poor kids were all frightened and bewildered. One little girl was so upset she started to cry and then wet her pants.

I found out later their hasty departure was to the bank to see if they could salvage anything. It was to no avail. The banks had already locked their doors."
- BB - Michigan

.   .   .

THE WEST

"I was a teenager in the 1930's. My family was certainly what would be considered "poor", but far from poverty-stricken. My recollection is that we were unaware that we were poor, perhaps because all our neighbors were similarly situated. There was not always money for things we wanted and sometimes not for things we needed. My father owned his own small printing business and income was sporadic and not something that could be budgeted.

Sometimes supper was corn meal mush (which I ate with sugar and butter melting on it). Because it was one of my favorite meals, I was not ever aware that it was inexpensive. A wonderful side benefit of hot corn meal mush was breakfast the following morning when the cold, leftover mush was sliced and fried and served with syrup. I felt it was truly a food for the gods!

Some of my best-loved clothing were hand-me-downs from the daughter of a doctor. I cannot remember ever being embarrassed to meet Mary Ruth in the hall at school when I was wearing a dress or pair of shoes that had been inherited from her.

During my junior year in high school, I had a date for the prom, but no prom dress. My date and I went anyhow and sat on the bleachers of the school gym to watch the dancers. My date did not dance, and I think I probably hoped the girls in long prom dresses thought that was the reason we were dressed informally and were there only as onlookers. I do not recall any great embarrassment over this, and am sure no tears were shed because circumstances were such that I did not have a prom dress.

One incident that stands out in my mind occurred in the mid-1930's. My father trudged the two miles home from work one evening bearing a pottery pitcher. It was yellow with blue trim. It was surely something we did not need, and something he had spent a half-dollar for that could have been used elsewhere to good advantage. My father had seen it in a store window and could not resist!

My mother was less than happy about this extravagance and was not hesitant to express her outrage. However, the displeasure was short-lived and the yellow and blue pitcher is still around! It graced my parent's home for many years, then came to live with me, and now reposes at my daughter's home where she loves to regale her friends with the history of the old yellow and blue pitcher. Time has shown that half-dollar was money well-spent!"

- BBM, South Dakota

.   .   .

"My grandfather raised eleven children and he never owned a thing or had a job. He was a sharecropper and turned over half of his produce to the owner of the land for the price of using the land. I remember that no part of an animal was wasted when they were slaughtered at my grandfather's home.

My father and mother lived in a mill town. My mother was a housewife and tended the gardens where we got our vegetables. We also had chickens and a cow. When the chickens did not lay, we did not have any eggs. We had meat only once a week, and we were happy just to have any kind of food to eat at all. There was no favorite food or meal in our household.

My father was a mechanic and truck driver for the mill. There were four trucks that delivered lumber during the day, and when they returned, it was my father's job to keep them up as well as drive a truck delivery during the day. There were many times when he would come home at midnight only to rise at three to go to work.

The county where we lived was a dry county. No liquor was bought or sold. My father would bootleg alcohol back to the county on some of his return trips in the state. There were also times when he would drive lumber to the coast and arrange to pick up oysters for those who could pay as part of the return trip. People would come and get their share, and we would get the oysters leftover at the bottom of the barrel. I remember that was very good eating for us.

We rarely ever saw any real money. Because it was a mill town, there was a company store where people picked up their basic needs and things were put on account. Maybe at the end of the week, my father would see one dollar.

I was born during the period of the great depression. When I turned six in 1937, I had to have my tonsils removed. The total cost of the operation was $35. It took the family three years to pay for it at fifty cents a week.

- CM - Texas

•   •   •

"We lived in a little town called Egan. My dad had a truck and he used to deliver coal and freight to homes and stores locally. We were very, very poor. Mom always had a garden and did a lot of canning. She could always make something out of nothing. I do not ever remember being hungry so I am sure she did a good job.

We lived in a lot of different houses. I don't know if we were moving up or could not afford the rent. My parents did the best they could.

I remember, when going to school in first grade, my aunt made me a jumper and the blouse had a large voile collar. A boy behind me at school scribbled all over it with his pencil. I was really upset. The last day of school I came home with a huge bottle of cod liver oil. Mother put it in everything she could think of to get me to take it, but I could always smell it first so I did not get much of that.

Dad also got a goat about that time, too. I don't think I ever liked goat milk either. I had to hold the goat up by the tail because she would not sit down while he milked her.

My brother, Chuck, was born in 1931 and another brother, Dick, in 1936. Both births were at home. Mother was not well when carrying Chuck. She could not keep food on her stomach and lived on malt the last month.

My aunt came for a few days when Dick was born and my sister and I thought she was mean because she would not let us hold him enough. It was later on, we got enough holding.

Dad would go to the coal yard and load up a 1/2 ton or ton of coal and deliver it to the homes and unload it into their basements or wherever they wanted it. The delivery charge was 50 cents. People did not always pay him at the time. So, I would have to go and try to collect. I look back now and find it hard to believe that a kid between eight and ten was sent to do this. Maybe that is why I now have a hard time asking for anything.

When the sweet corn was ripe, we would go around town selling it so that we could all go to a tent show that was in town. I know we sold it real cheap. I believe it was two cents a cob. I also remember selling cottage cheese that mother made. Another thing we had for sale were big beefsteak tomatoes that mom and dad had grown. They were hard to sell at 50 cents a bushel already picked.

During this time, dad had a little model "T" truck with no top on the cab. He delivered ice to homes in the summer. In the evening, we would take turns steering and the others pushing. We had more fun with that truck. It was so lightweight.

In 1934, my grandfather died at Lake Campbell. It was about 35 miles from Egan and in those days that was quite a drive. The coffin was in the living room and a service was held there. I do not remember if they went to the church for another service. I remember my cousin saying "Grandpa's here now, but he's going to heaven." It was very strange and sad.

Several times during this time, my uncle would stop by on his way to my uncle's farm at Lake Campbell. I believe he was coming from Iowa. He was a single man and he always had a big bag of candy. It was so exciting and was like having Santa Claus visit. One time, he stopped and he had a woman with him. He had gotten married and we never got anymore visits or goodies anymore.

The railroad came through Egan, and in the winter, the engine would be covered with snow. I was in awe of it. In the summer, there were hoboes who would stop and ask for food. If mom could, she would make them a sandwich, or if she had baked, she would give them fresh bread or cake. They sometimes would offer to do odd jobs, but I think she mostly wanted them to go on their way. If they got too much, they came back, and I don't think my parents trusted them.

In the mid 1930's, my father got work on the WPA. They then did a lot of community work on highways, parks, etc. The wages were $44 a month.

He worked on a project at the city park. They built picnic tables, benches, and a bath house from cement and different size stones. They were really nice.

In 1990, we returned to the park. It was deserted, but those stone tables and building were still there. The park is on the Sioux river.

When you were on relief (WPA), you were eligible for food and clothing. Every month, they would deliver food. I think dad helped with the food delivery. There were lots of raisins. In fact, we had so much raisin pie that I cannot eat it now. There were also canned meats and corn meal.

For the clothing, we had to go to the county seat. My sister and I would get dresses. They were new but very plain. I think they took three patterns and three different prints and got groups to sew them. If someone had a dress with the same print, you knew where they got it.

Once my sister got a lovely wool snowsuit. The only one they had in my size was corduroy. I always froze in it, but my sister was warm and cozy in hers. I was tall for my age and had to settle for what would fit.

In the late 1930's, we started getting a Christmas box from our aunt in Iowa. She would send clothes that her daughters did not want anymore. That was very exciting for us.

When my grandfather died, my father inherited 80 acres of land. His brother and nephew farmed it, and after the harvest, dad would get his share of the grain money. I suspect that helped pay up any outstanding bills and got a few things that were needed.

My parents had several couples they played cards with, and they played "Five Hundred" a lot. Sometimes, on Sundays, we would drive to Lake Campbell to visit uncles, aunts, and cousins. There was always lots of good food and fun to be had. We would also visit some aunts in Madison.

In the summer, dad would go downtown and visit with the men. We would decide to walk down and see if he would give us a penny. If he had some, he would give us one. You could get a pretty good treat for a penny.

In early 1939, we moved back to Lake Campbell. Dad worked for farmers and did odd jobs. I think the wages were about $10 a week. In the winter, he cut ice at the lake for the ice house that stored it for summer use. The wages were $1.50 a day.

Mother had some chickens and sold eggs to the little store at the lake. I remember taking a dozen eggs and getting a pound of hamburger in return. We would fry the hamburger and make a good gravy from the potatoes we had stored for the winter.

Most homes had a cellar to store the food for the winter, and cisterns that stored rain water for bathing. Sometimes you could put food in a bucket and tie a rope to the handle and hang it down the cistern to keep cool. The family was always coming up with new ways to keep things cool.

Back in the country, we went to a one-room school. They usually had a basement where the furnace was and where we could play in the winter. All eight grades were together. Each grade had about two or three kids, and if there was only one child for a grade, they would study with either the lower or upper grade, whichever the teacher thought they could do.

My sister and I always worked in the summer taking care of kids or helping wives with their daily chores. You would get fifty cents a week from relatives and $2 a week from other families.

I had some jobs I really liked and some did not last over a week. I would stay from Sunday night until Saturday night. I only had one day off. I believe the five-day week came a lot later in life.

Two summers in a row, I worked for couples where the wife was pregnant. I washed dishes and the milk separator and helped with cooking, laundry, cleaning house, weeding the garden, and baking. You name it and I did it.

One lady I worked for had a two year old boy when she went to the hospital to deliver a new baby. I had to do all the work alone. I took care of the house, cooked for two men, gardened, looked after the little boy, and shopped for groceries. I got $4 a week for this and thought I was rich.

Dad's work was mostly for farmers. My sister's and my work was for farm wives. My mother had a cousin who had a big, square two-story farmhouse. Mother would go clean it on Saturdays. During the fall season, the cousin would entertain neighbors and mother would clean and make oyster stew for her dinner. I believe mother got $1.50.

When I was a freshman in high school, I had to walk three miles to catch the bus to go to school twenty miles from home. That was really tough sometimes. It was often 30 degrees below zero and quite often windy. With the cold and snow, we hardly ever used the car so we had to walk. We could not afford antifreeze so it was a big job to get the car started.

When we lived in the country, we did not have electricity. We used kerosene or gas lamps, and we had to do laundry by hand with a scrub board or a tub that had a handle that rocked it like a cradle. We had to take turns pushing the handle back and forth. Some people had gas washing machines, but we could not afford that luxury. You had to heat the water on the cook stove in an oblong tub, and then pour it into the machine or wash tub. It took a man to handle the job or else we dipped it from one to the other.

We also had the outhouse and had to bring water from a well outside. We always had a bucket and dipper on a bench for drinking and a big bucket nearby as a slop bucket for waste water and garbage that would be emptied out where the chickens and animals were.

The winters were the hardest to survive. There were not a lot of trees in the area. We burned a lot of corn cobs and coal. The stove was a monster in the living room and the stove pipes went through a hole in the ceiling and through the second floor bedroom and then through to the chimney. That was how the upstairs was heated. We sometimes heated the iron bases and wrapped in a towel and took them to bed to warm our feet. (We have come a long way, baby, since then!)

Most of the social events were in the school or church. In the summer, we would go to town and try to park on main street. This way you got to see the neighbors and us kids would get to play and sometimes go to a movie while the adults visited. This was Saturday night fun.

On Sunday afternoon, we would go the lake. There was a big roller skating ring, cafe, beer parlor, and swimming there. The adults would play cards while us kids played and sometimes mother would play the piano and sing Norwegian songs to us. We did not have a radio very often because we could not afford batteries. Most times you went to bed early in the winter to save on the lamps.

In 1943, our family moved to Washington state. It was quite a shock to move to a big city compared to rural South Dakota. Our first experience was six-lane roads compared to a two-lane road and lots of buses."

\- AMG - South Dakota

.   .   .

"My most vivid memory of the Depression was that we were married on June 12, 1929. My sister and I had a double wedding at my parent's home. There were no photographers or florists, but we had lots of garden flowers from Dad's garden. Mother had a dinner after the ceremony. The girls had pretty new dresses and the boys had new suits, but there was no formal wear.

I went to live in Hastings, Nebraska where my husband had a Post Office job. We rented a brand new bungalow for $37.50 a month.

My husband was a substitute at the Post Office for the first couple of years and our time was spent getting the house furnished and starting the lawn. The third year, we built a brick home and had a baby daughter. Our daughter's arrival in the world was my happiest moment.

Holidays were mainly celebrated by having family dinners. Our happiest holiday was the first Christmas in our new home with our brand new baby.

When the family became ill, I took care of them. I did not work and took them to the doctor or had the doctor come out to the house.

We did not have many dress-up clothes, but always managed several outfits of work and every day wear. I washed every Monday and ironed every Tuesday so we would be sure to have clean clothes for the week.

We knew of many young men who could not find work and there were others who had had jobs but got laid off. I helped a few strangers who came to the back door asking for food.

My favorite meal was roast beef dinner, but most often I cooked hamburger in many, different ways.

My worst meal was one day when I looked up from my housework and saw my sister and her three little girls and her friend with two more little girls drive up just before noon. I knew I only had 50 cents in the house, but was saved by our garden. I made potato and onion soup, and we had rhubarb sauce for dessert.

Our saddest moment was when my husband got laid off for a month from the Post Office. However, one of the other men at the Post Office had my husband paint a house for him so we got by.

I believe my husband worried more than I did about finances during those years, but I always prayed each night for God's help in raising our family and keeping the home going. We never blamed God for our troubles."

- Nebraska

.   .   .

"My most vivid memory of the Depression was terrible dust storms, economic depression, and my 1935 marriage! My marriage was my happiest moment and it was held outdoors.

I paid cash for things that I wanted and often patronized thrift shops for used items. When family became ill, we mostly took care of ourselves. It was very seldom we used doctors."

- Colorado

.   .   .

"The Depression was a time when families were close. Children grew up surrounded with love from parents, grandparents, aunts, uncles and cousins. We had fun together. We respected our parents and grandparents. Old or young, everyone in the family pitched in to do whatever needed to be done.

In my family, during this time, was my grandfather, aunt, several uncles, my mother and my sister. Our big meal was in the evening, and we had lively discussions, but always on a pleasant note.

I remember being sent from the table one time when I was sarcastic with my aunt. I could not return until I could say something nice.

My mother always managed to do something a little special for the holidays. Christmas was my favorite time. We opened our gifts on Christmas Eve. Mother made most of the gifts as money was scarce, but there was always something.

She hid eggs for Easter, and we had fun hunting them on Easter morning. Thanksgiving was a family affair with a big turkey. I can still remember mother getting up at 4:00 a.m. to put the turkey in the oven. She always made several kinds of pie and homemade rolls. Wonderful smells came from that kitchen!

We had simple meals, but they were always well-balanced and good. Meat was a treat. We ate a lot of creamed eggs, macaroni and cheese, oyster stew, beans, etc.

One experience I have never forgotten was going shopping with my mother. She bought a large roast at the meat market which was probably meant to last for several meals. We then went to Woolworth's before we went home. I was carrying the package of meat while we looked around the store. We got about half-way home when I realized I didn't have the package. I ran all the way back to the store afraid the package would be gone. Thank goodness, it was still there. I wonder if that would hold true today?

We lived near a small grocery store where we would charge our groceries and pay at the end of each month. On rare occasions, I would get a nickel for candy, and I would spend agonizing moments standing before the candy case trying to decide which penny candy I wanted. I loved the spearmint leaves.

Most of my clothes were made by my mother. She was a very, clever seamstress. She would see something in the department store window and go home and make it. I never felt like my clothes looked homemade. It would have been unthinkable to wear jeans to school. Jeans was something one put on after school.

My sister and I shared the same bedroom. We did not have many outfits and therefore did not complain about not having enough closet space.

We played many card games around the dining room table. Monopoly was a favorite game. Saturday was a special day as my sister and I got to go to a show. It cost the whole sum of 10 cents and for that we got to see a double feature movie, a serial, the news, and they always had a drawing for prizes. We were usually pretty lucky, but I would never go up on stage to claim my prize. I would make my sister go. This was at the Mayan Theater in Denver, and it is still in operation.

A lot of us who lived through the 1930's really did not know we were poor. A lot of people were all in the same boat. It did not take money for the family to have fun together."

- BLD - Colorado

.   .   .

"As a young girl, aged ten to fourteen, I never even knew anything was different about the times of the Depression. I realize now that my parents must have worried, but all six of their children (four boys and two girls) were happy as larks. We had a happy family. We lived in the mountains in Rattlesnake Park. (The B.L.M. took part of the meadow and made a lake out of it in 1950. It is now called Pinewood Lake.)

During the Depression, we had drought, cold winters, and lots of wind. The wind blew the soil away from the grass and alfalfa, During recess and lunchtime, we school kids would go out and look and found many arrowheads.

When the swamp froze over, we ice-skated. Sometimes, we pulled the horse buggy by hand up to the top of Bald Mountain and coasted down. Some of us got hurt when we fell off and the wheel ran over us.

We walked to school. It was a mile and a half, and so we got plenty of fresh air. Many of the trees on the Blue and Green Mountain blew down so we had plenty of wood to keep us warm.

We always had a big Thanksgiving and Christmas dinner. We raised our own chickens and turkeys. We always had a nice birthday cake and plenty to eat. Sometimes, we had to take cold pancakes for lunch or homemade bread with sugar and thick cream on it. It was very good and I liked sugar.

Mother sold eggs to the grocery store and sour cream to the creamery. A dollar went a long ways then.

In the fall, before school started, mother would take us to Penny's and we all got a pair of shoes, the boys some overalls, and the girls a dress. That was usually it for the year.

Sometimes, an aunt, who lived in Denver, would send up a box of clothes that she was through with. Mother made me and my sister a jacket out of two big men's bathrobes. They were very pretty.

If anyone came to our house, the folks always would invite them to eat with us. Mother fed many neighbors, and dad loved to visit. Their stories were precious. Mother used to open the window so she could listen. Dad had four brothers, and when they got together, it was a "Do-You-Remember" time. They were all raised up in the area.

The year 1932 was no doubt a bad year for my parents. Dad did not have a job and Mother lost a baby in January.

We raised a big garden, had our milk cow and chickens, and wild plum and chokeberry jelly. They would buy 100 pounds of sugar and flour in the fall and a 50 pound lard can. I will always remember those fluffy biscuits my mother made.

If any of us became ill, our mother took care of us the best she could. We had a lot of earaches and sore throats. We were all grown when we got the measles, chicken-pox, and the mumps.

In 1933, dad got a good job. Before this, he had always been a cattle rancher. In the depression years, the government paid you $20 and then shot the starving cattle. It was very sad.

Dad was hired as the shop man for a new road up the Thompson canyon. He sharpened tools (picks, shovels, bars and all sorts of machinery that needed fixing.) He and mother joined the Democrat party and went dancing again. When the road was finished, the Depression was over, and we were all back into ranching again.

In 1935, my sister and I and three of my brothers were working in the hayfields. We were paid 50 cents a day for racking and driving the stacker team.

My oldest brother made $1 a day for mowing the hay. He was the big shot. You know you could buy a lot with a dollar."

- RLE - Colorado

.　　　.　　　.

"We lived in Kansas during the Depression, and I vividly remember the dust storms.

My happiest day was my wedding day in July, 1936. We had it in church, but it was very simple. We received household items as gifts. We did not have many outfits during those days and received both new and used things.

My favorite holiday was Thanksgiving when we would have a big family gathering."

- Kansas

.　　　.　　　.

"When my husband had vacations, we would drive all night to go see his folks in Arvada. We drove all night because we could not afford a motel. We would stay long enough to save on food, services, etc., and we always came back loaded with milk, eggs, chickens, and other things from the farm.

One day, we were going down to Colfax on our way back home. Everyone waved or honked at us. We decided all the attention was because they had never seen a Missouri license plate.

Then, someone came at us with a fire extinguisher. We had a box on our running board filled with grease rags. When Earl dumped ashes from his pipe over the side of the car, it had set the rags on fire. Harry, who was with us, jumped out of the car and dumped all our fresh milk on the fire. So, we made the trip home with no milk from the farm, and the fire had caused no major damage.

From Springfield to Arvada, there were very few hard top or gravel roads. From Salina, Kansas west, we had dirt roads only. There were many times the roads were mud and required chains on all four wheels. We followed other cars in the ruts, and Harry loved to take off his shoes and wade in the mud to help push other cars ahead of us that were stuck. This was the most fun especially if the helpless car was a Cadillac.

Purina moved their salesmen often. (We moved 22 times in nine years.) They were always giving them new territories to develop. Times were getting tough and we were moved to Illinois. We were there for three years and it was here that our neighbor started my daughter on a quarter-size violin. She taught her for 15 minutes a day and would not allow me to watch the lesson or her to bring her fiddle home. That was the start of what is now my child's professional career.

We enjoyed Matton as they had a wonderful basketball team with a very talented star. This star later became a pro, but I cannot remember his name.

We also made our first trip to Yellow stone driving from Matton. We stayed in Tourist courts and in those days, we always had to carry along our own bedding and towels.

In Yellow stone, the "Boys" rapped on our cabin door very early, came in with oiled shavings, and started a fire in our little stove so that it would be warm when we got up. The Park was very different then. Near Canyon Village, they put the autos and the people in a fenced-in area and spread the hotel garbage in the valley below for the bears to eat. On some nights we would only see one or two bears, but then on the next night, we might see 30 to 40. We often saw them fighting and heard awful roars. Once we saw a bear come out of the Yellow stone Lake with a huge fish in its mouth. It crossed the road in front of us and went on into the woods. Another time, we met a bear with three cubs (one blonde, one brunette and one redhead). We wondered if she was a bad girl!

We also saw the beautiful Tetons. Several years later, we had a family party on Jackson Lake looking up to the Tetons. We rented a big boat with a guide. It was wonderful fishing and wonderful days.

We then moved to Illinois. We raised chickens in our attic for meat. Then, all Purina salesmen were eliminated and we were out of a job.

We went to Arvada and stayed with my husband's folks for a few weeks until Earl got a new job with Quaker Oats. This time we moved to Des Moines, Iowa. We found a good violin teacher for Betty, my daughter. We had to enroll her in Drake University to be eligible for this teacher to teach her, and so our daughter, at age 6, was the youngest student ever enrolled in the University.

Just a few months later, Earl's former boss at Purina called and begged him to come to Chicago to interview for a job. Earl went, got the job, and the banks went "broke" on that very same day, March 6, 1933. Fortunately, he had his train ticket home and $10 in his pocket.

We moved to the Chicago area. We moved first to Rogers Park where Betty was ready for first grade. Then, Earl discovered Negro children in their schools and he said, "No Way." So, we moved to Evanston to a better school, but Evanston was too expensive and we moved again to Glen Ellen, Illinois.

On Easter Sunday, 1933, I had a sudden lung hemorrhage. It was tuberculosis! Because our home had an attached sleeping porch, I was allowed to stay home on that porch, providing my children never entered my quarters.

We had a wonderful "live-in" lady who took care of my children, did all the housework, and cooked all the meals. She also kept all of my food, dishes, laundry, and all personal things separate, and I did not use the family bathroom. The children were taken to Wyoming for the summer. My daughter, Betty, wrote me every day and I have saved those letters.

There was no known medicine for tuberculosis. Treatment consisted of long-term bed rest.

I was fed three big meals a day with cream to drink between meals. I was also required to consume three pounds of butter each week.

Once a month, Earl took me to a Sanatorium for evaluation and they always said I was doing fine and to come back in 30 days. I gained a lot of weight. My only amusement was an aquarium of tropical fish and baseball games on the radio.

On one trip home from the sanatorium, I was very discouraged. Earl bought me a new fish. It was a "Black Molly." It was a tropical fish and was very pregnant. This type of fish gives birth to live babies rather than eggs. They were born that night, and we had a wonderful time staying up way into the night to watch the births.

During this year with tuberculosis, I also had Whooping Cough with the kids. They were never allowed on my porch, but I still got it.

While I was fighting Whooping Cough, my appendix ruptured. Because of my condition, the operation had to be performed without any anesthetic.

When Earl returned to the office the next morning, the boss called him in and said, "Earl, you have had enough! Bring me the bill for her operation." Also, our close friends had a brand new car with a trunk. A trunk was a new gadget on a car. They gave the car to Earl to use for transportation to and from the hospital which was seven miles away.

When I was out of bed and getting my strength back, the boss sent Earl on a business trip West and told him to take me along with all expenses paid. On that trip, we visited his folks and they gave me a Toy Boston Terrier puppy we named Mickey. After being so long in bed, I could not stand having a lot of activity around. Mickey curled up on my lap and was very calming. I soon got back my old pep and life was great.

I fully recovered in one year. However, Esther, my sister, had made the choice not to take care of herself. She wanted to raise her boys first. She died in a sanatorium in 1938.

We then moved to a big house with a third story attic. We had a big Halloween party up in that attic. One of our guests was delayed and arrived late. As he walked into the living room en route to the party upstairs, he discovered a decoration on the fireplace mantel was on fire and flaming up the wall. He yelled at all of us and we all got out safely while they put out the fire.

Mr. Harker died unexpectedly in 1935, and my husband was moved up into his job. This meant we participated in company profits.

We bought our first house that year. Times were still very hard. A bank in Wisconsin offered an eight-room house with full basement and attic, on a 150-foot square lot for the long over-do mortgage of $4,900. We bought it. It was a block from school and close to a fancy country club with a beautiful 18-hole golf course. In 1992, the taxes on that house was more than what we had paid for it.

The house was in excellent condition. We had fun decorating and fixing it up. We put a recreation room in the basement and my son, Bob, put his train set with "miles" of track in the attic. He and his little neighbor friend spent hours up there.

During these years, I ran a veritable taxi. I took my husband to the train station every day, the kids to school and music lessons, and me to church affairs.

In 1936, Earl's mother died in February in Colorado. She was buried in Missouri, and our trip from Chicago to the funeral was made on glare ice. Social security began during this year.

Earls' dad had a little Overland car. When he got lonesome he would drive and live with us until he got mad at us. Then, he would drive to Wyoming to live with Earl's sister until he got mad at them. Then, he would drive back to see us. He sold his Colorado property and just spent his time going back and forth between his two children until he died in 1944.

On one drive to us, he fell asleep behind the wheel and landed in the middle of a pasture. There was no damage, but he was scared. When he arrived at our house, he gave Earl the keys and said he would never drive again. After that, he took the train.

We had lots of friends in Glen Ellen. Earl commuted to the Chicago Loop every day on the Aurora and Elgin trains that used the "L" tracks around the Loop. I loved to ride the "L" into Marshall Fields to window shop. I was very active in the church as Secretary-Treasurer of the Ladies Aid and Chairman of a church Circle. We also had a bridge club and played lots of cards.

During this time we also got a weaned St. Bernard dog. It was so big we had quite a time taking it on the train back into Chicago. It took some bribes. We loved this dog which we called "Duke." In one years time, he grew until he was as tall as Earl when he stood on his hind legs. He was very lovable and he loved Mickey, the other dog. We called them "Mutt and Jeff."

In 1936, some friends came from California to stay with us until he found a job. One day, we decided to have a twelfth birthday party for my son and his friends in the basement. We made a cake shaped like a big ship and had red popsicles on it. Our recreation room had new white walls before the party, but after the party, we had red polka dot walls where the kids had played darts with red poker chips.

Our friends soon moved to Lombard, Illinois which was five miles away. We spent lots of time together.

The school kids loved Duke and Mickey as they walked by our house. Duke was confined to our large lot. The elderly neighbors, who lived back of us, felt Duke was too confined. They felt so sorry for him that one night they poisoned him. Mickey was a house dog at night. So, thankfully, he did not get poisoned.

Since our house was large, we had Grandma Tobey living with us as well as my parents until they moved to Philadelphia.

During this period, we made a trip West each summer. We always included the Tetons and Yellow stone. All the roads were now gravel or paved. There were no more mud roads. Our tourist courts were becoming motels with linen included most of the time and road maps became available.

In 1937, my mother came to Glen Ellen for a visit and we planned a trip West for our vacation. In order to lengthen Earl's two-week vacation, mother and I took the children and drove to Denver on Thursday and Friday. Then, Earl and daddy took the train in Chicago on Friday night. We met them Saturday morning in Greeley, Colorado.

Mother had always wanted to see "Mile High" Denver. I decided to surprise her. Instead of driving into Denver, I drove west to a road in the foothills that took us to Lookout Mountain which is high above the city. I drove to a vantage point overlooking Denver and said, "Now, Mama, there is Denver down there."

She said, "No! It could not be Denver because Denver was a mile high." I am afraid I burst her dream, but she enjoyed telling the story many times.

When Esther died in 1938, we took the children into our home until her husband could pick up his life again and make a home. We had lots of fun with four kids. Their ages were 15, 12, 11 and 9. I was only 33 and looked like I was 21, so I got stared at many times with these four children.

One day, we were all going up the escalator in the big Marshall Fields in downtown Chicago. My son got his tennis shoe caught in the escalator step. The whole escalator ripped from top to bottom and stopped. We created much attention, but no one was hurt. They gave the kids ice cream cones and sent us on our way.

When my sister, Esther, died, the shock of losing her "first born" was more than my mother could handle. She became so depressed that the doctor told my father if she did not find a hobby she would go insane.

Mother had been an artist in her very early days. So, daddy told her he wished she would paint him a picture of a road with the colorful trees in the fall. She immediately got out a canvas and oils and began to paint. It opened up a new world to her, and she left us with approximately 75 wonderful oil paintings.

In 1939, we took the children on an educational trip to Washington, D.C., New York City, and down the beautiful Blue Ridge Parkway. My uncle, Walter, turned over his apartment in New York for us to use while in New York City."

- DGM - Illinois and Colorado

•　　　•　　　•

"I grew up on a cattle ranch in Wyoming. I could not see much difference in our situation. I went to college with very few clothes and graduated just before the Depression got underway. One thing that stands out in my mind is that when I left my job in the mid-1930's, I was getting less salary than when I began.

There were the usual WPE's, CCC (Civilian Conservation Corps) and a real curtailment in travel. Most of the people I worked with lived in rural areas and many were self-employed. They produced their own food and there was not as much need or want as in the cities.

I was married in 1936 in a simple wedding. My husband worked for the U.S. Government in a relief program, but in agricultural areas.

One memory I have is of my supervisor suggesting it may be better if I would buy some new clothes. I was paying education debts and for a car that was necessary for travel which seemed more important to me than new clothes."

- Wyoming

.　　　.　　　.

"The Garfield Street house in Lincoln, Nebraska was a two-story, yellow frame with a spacious pantry and kitchen. We had our breakfast at a white enameled table. Mother also used this as her work table because the kitchen did not have counters or cupboards other than the pantry shelves.

There was a walk-through coat closet connecting the kitchen and the front hall. This closet was often used by Dad pacing back door to front door, back and forth, while he worked out a problem in his mind.

Mother kept her sewing machine in the dining room. She always had some mending or a sewing project under way. When we girls took Home Economics at school, we began using the machine also. Our round, oak dining table, with extensions in place, became the layout and cutting table between meals. My twin sister and I made simple housecoats which led us to try more complicated patterns.

The rule of the house was we had to wear whatever we started. It did not matter what the results were. I remember a pair of culottes I made were an embarrassment when I had to wear them to one of Dad's softball games. I had misread the pattern instruction and cut off what I took to be surplus material in one leg in this full-split-skit, type fashion. I ended up with one leg of the skirt nice and full and the other leg skimpy. My twin sister's culottes turned out just fine because of my horrible example.

Our living room was the gathering place after supper. One of us would do homework at the small oak, drop-leaf desk while the other of us reading books from the glass front bookcase. Dad would be seated in his green, easy chair with his long legs stretched out to the matching footstool having a brief look at the newspaper before going back to the shop for the rest of the night. My Aunt Dilla's tapestry covered the sofa. Another easy chair, floor lamps, and lace curtains completed the decor in this room.

There were four children in the family. We helped Mother garden in the back yard. We raised a lot of our own food because this was a necessity during the Depression. (Later, during World War II, Victory Gardens were a patriotic duty. Even window box gardens in apartments were considered Victory Gardens.).

There were three small bedrooms and a bathroom upstairs. Gail, Jean and Jane's bedroom had a long, low, dark, slant-ceiling closet where we went to sulk when any of us was disciplined. Spankings and switchings were frequent rites of passage and most often were administered with ceremony and a lecture by our father at the supper table.

The basement contained a gas furnace. This was a luxury for Mother who had shoveled coal for years before Cy was old enough to help. There was a hand-wound phonograph on which we played Caruso and Lawrence Tibbets records on rainy days.

One corner of the basement was furnished with an old couch and an oak wash stand. Dad lived in the cool corner for several weeks one summer after he had a heat stroke while installing an antenna on a customer's roof. The crew from the shop assembled before him each morning to get their orders for the day, and we children carried additional messages to and from Dad the rest of the day. Mother's trips up and down the stairs to minister to Dad's needs were countless.

Other calamities that befell Dad while we lived at the house were stomach ulcers which plagued him for years and an incident of being overcome by refrigeration gas. The continuing struggle to survive the Great Depression to feed, clothe, shelter and educate his family no doubt contributed to his vulnerability to accidents and illness.

My father's financially hard-up customers would pay him with barter of trade-off in services or other things. The system worked the other way also. If one of us needed medical or dental attention, Dad would repay the services with car, radio, small appliance or refrigeration service.

One time, this exchange of resources resulted in a lasting pleasure for all of us. A customer traded a dark brown, male springer-and-water spaniel. Dad named the dog Rudyard Kipling Gunga Din Ginger. We immediately shortened it to "Kip."

Kip developed into a fine hunting dog, guard god and charming family pet. His guarding instincts came into play mainly when the garbage man was on his biweekly rounds or when a tramp approached the back yard in the vain hopes of getting to the back door to ask Mother for something to eat.

One day, Aunt Dilla called Dad and begged him to stop everything and bring Kip to find her Pekingese. The Pekingese was named "Fon Li". Fon Li was a very, real member of the household. When he decided to run across the street into a acres-large cemetery, panic set in.

Dad interrupted his work and sped across town with Kip. Dad later return to report that Kip had successfully tracked down the Pekingese and wore the little dog out after a spirited chase among the headstone. Then, Dad caught Fon Li and returned him safely to Aunt Dilla's arms.

During the summer of 1934/1935, we began to experience the effects of the dust bowl. The awful dust blew through our town for week after long week. We were all in a state of suspended animation. Nothing thrived. There was no daylight. All outdoor activity was drastically curtailed. Water usage for baths, lawns, gardens and other non-essential use was prohibited. The heat wave continued, but no doors or windows stood open lest the dust cover all belongings, including food cooking on the stove.

Fourth of July:

Our favorite family outings were picnics. These were usually at Antelope Park in Lincoln. Less frequently were picnics at Capitol Beach where there was a salt-water swimming pool fed by the nearby river. I also have fond memories of night trips on the Fourth of July to watch breathtaking fireworks from the roadside at the beach.

While Grandma Duffie and Great Grandpa Mahan were alive, we spent Sunday evenings at their house on 35th & Q. Makeshift tables were set up in the side yard for the children while the adults ate a potluck, picnic supper indoors.

We twins felt honored that Uncle Curtis opted to eat with us even after he qualified by age to be indoors with the adults. The children were always the last to be served. By the time it came to be our turn, we were usually sick from waiting so long or from laughing so hard at Uncle Curtis's antic.

Before sparklers and fireworks were brought out, someone would make a phone call to the corner drug store. Soon, there were cartons of delicious strawberry and chocolate ice cream. These would be delivered and ladled into small, glass dishes.

At sundown, we all sang "The Star Spangled Banner" while Great Grandpa lowered the flag from the pole in the center of the front yard. Then, Dad was kept busy as supervisor of the excited sparkler bearers and as chief igniter of the fantastic sky rockets. This required great agility and eyes in the back of his head. Fourth of July was often the occasion for a visit by Wyoming and California cousins.

May Day:

May Day was a delightful rite of spring. We celebrated it at school and at home.

At the elementary school, we laid plans for a jitney lunch and a May Pole dance. Our teachers' enthusiasm for this special time was like catching a case of the measles.

The jitney lunch required the cooperation of the mothers. They were asked to bring a main dish or desert to be served in nickle-a-piece portions from long tables set up in the hallways. On May Day, nothing was done on a as-usual basis. The cafeteria was closed. No tests were given. Students wore their Sunday best. Fathers prepared to dig into their pockets for nickels for each of their children. Mothers tied the nickels in the corner of hankies for safekeeping. By mid-morning, the mothers and a few fathers began arriving with the home-cooked dishes. The fathers helped janitors set up the tables and the mother assisted the teachers in serving the meal and collecting the nickels as each class filed past the tables.

It was all a wonderful treat. Normally, we children would always walk home for lunch in all kinds of weather.

After lunch, everyone gathered in the courtyard where tall, metal poles had been erected. There were seven poles altogether with one for each grade. Each pole had long, pastel crepe paper streamers attached to a ring at the top. Upon a signal and to the accompaniment of a piano, each child would grasp a streamer and dance around the pole. This would continue until the streamers were intertwined in a variegated pattern of colors. Then, the dancers reversed themselves until the streamers hung straight again and were ready for the next group of dancers. It was a wonderful kaleidoscope with seven colorful May Poles all going at once.

Afterwards, the parents dispersed and the children returned to the classroom to tell their favorite May Day event. Classes were dismissed early, and we hurried home to put the finishing touches on May baskets.

May baskets were made of colored construction paper. We began getting our materials together at least a week before May Day. We made paste with flour and water, cut the colored paper into squares or rectangles, formed corners by snipping in an inch or two on all sides, and then pasting two strips over each other until they formed a box. A strip of the same paper was pasted at two sides opposite each other making the handle. Each of us made several May baskets for friends. My twin sister and I were only allowed on basket between us per friend. We did not mind this since we shared most of the same friends.

A day or two ahead of time, Mother would take us hunting for flowers, such as violets and lilacs. On May Day, we helped Mother and Gail make fudge and popcorn. After an early supper, we arranged the fudge, popcorn, and flowers in each basket. Then, at dusk, we would steal to the front door of each friends, set a basket down, rap on the door, and hide behind the nearest tree where we could see and hear the reaction of whoever opened the door. What squeals and giggles! Oddly, I only remember giving of May baskets. I do not remember receiving any. However, the true, real pleasure was in the carrying out of this tradition for our German and Russian descended neighbors and friends.

Even as little children, we appreciated that our parents were somehow able to provide the resources, no matter how simple, for us to participate in activities such as May Day and Valentines Day. The nickels Dad distributed, the construction paper, and ingredients for duke were hard to come by during the Depression years.

Memorial Day:

Memorial Day involved us twins in a ceremony at Wyuka Cemetery. This was located across the street from Grandma and Great Grandpa's house. In the morning, Mother would dress us in our pale, green dressed with lace-trimmed ruffles and pink satin rose buds on black velvet bows. Our green socks matched the dresses and our pink satin-lined capes tied at the neck. Grandma and Mother worked together throughout preceding months making our outfits.

Dad and Mother droves us to get our grandparents and then drove through the huge, black iron gates of the cemetery. Great Grandpa, James Curtis Mahan, would take his place among the honored veterans of the Civil War, Spanish-American War and World War I. Speeches of respect for the living and dead heroes were given. Afterwards, everyone proceeded to the stone bridge over a meandering stream. While Taps was played in the morning, my sister and I sprinkled rose petals from baskets into the gently flowing water. White swans drifted on the stream.

After Great Grandpa's death, we girls would join Mother for a trip to Raymond, where we would pick up Mother's sister, Aunt Ethel, and go to the little cemetery there. While the two sisters tidied the graves of their parents and chatted about old times, we three girls browsed among the grassy mounds reading inscriptions on headstones. We also helped carry buckets of fresh, iris, peonies, and other seasonal flowers that our elders had picked early in the morning.

Halloween:

Halloween was another occasion for Dad and Mother to bring ingenuity into play. Dad showed Cy how to notch the ends of empty wooden spools to make rackety noisemakers when wound with twine. They would quickly unreel them against a neighbor's window.

Mother dug into her scrap bag for makings of costumes and disguises for her goblins. A bright orange. cardboard Jack'O Lantern, complete with candle, escorted us in the early dark as we hooted at other goblins going about in the neighborhood. Soaping windows was a permissible activity for the teenage boys. In fact, most housewives put off window washing until Halloween was over.

Thanksgiving:

Thanksgiving in Lincoln meant cold weather, very likely snow, and lots of home cooking. There were pumpkin for pies, turkey, dressing, mashed potatoes, giblet gravy, candied yams, homemade rolls, cranberry sauce, pickle-lily relish, whipped cream, and cold milk.

It also meant the aroma of Uncle Scott's and Dad's cigars. Uncle Scott would nudge me on one side of him and Jean on the other as we all perched on a long board placed across dining chairs in order to extend seating space at the table. We children always had some riddles ready for Uncle Scott so that we could watch him quake with laughter.

The day meant frosty gusts of air as the Lincoln relatives came in with their food offerings and hearty greetings. The adults visited in the front room sipping wine while Mother and we girls would put the finishing touches on the table and buffet.

Thanksgiving for me meant endlessly passing dishes and having an adult serve us. It meant feeling almost ill from too much food and good company. It meant stuporous conversation until we recovered enough to gather around the piano to sing while Aunt Dilla or Aunt Fanny played.

After dinner we cleared the table, washed dishes in the metal dishpan, scalded them in the sink with boiling water, and my sister and I dried them. Then, we stacked them on the table for an early evening snack before family departed. Often, there was a gigantic box of chocolates set out on the dining table. This was a rare after-dinner treat.

Christmas:

Christmas involved each of us four children in projects that results in gifts and decorations. Almost as soon as the last Thanksgiving drumstick was picked clean, Mother would get out colored paper, empty jars, scissors, paste, and shellac. We cut the paper in a variety of angles and triangles. Mother and Gail pasted them on the jars and added a coat of shellac. The result was stained glass containers which would be filled with hard candy or bath crystals for aunts and grandmas.

During the 1930's, there was no such thing as mass mailings of Christmas greetings. Such greetings were only sent by a few to out- of-town relatives. The few we received were displayed on our window sills where the heavily frosted panes provided an appropriate back-drop.

Popped corn and cranberries were strung into long ropes with needle and thread. Colored paper links were formed into endless chains and draped from corner to corner in the living and dining rooms.

Preparations were begun for a big family dinner to match all the glories of Thanksgiving. The turkey or goose had to be plucked, and Mother always stuffed and roasted it with unmatched success in her little gas stove.

We children saved a few pennies, and with weather permitting, would walk a mile and a half to downtown. We would browse through the dime store until we found just the right handkerchief for Uncle Scott.

One year, Grandma helped us embroider a hanky for Mother. We would walk three blocks to the streetcar line, ride to O Street and transfer to another line that took us within a block of Grandma's house.

On another Christmas, Jean and I managed to earn enough pennies to buy an initialed handkerchief for Uncle Scott and a small bottle of Lily of the Valley toilet water for Gail. We were excited and proud to be able to buy gifts for someone. We never gave gifts to each other because it seemed like you were giving yourself a present.

Mother and Dad received painted and shellacked hand prints from each of their children. We made these in school. I remember the smell and feel of the wet clay and the pride in the finished products with our names scratched in them. I can still feel the weights of this gift inside its tissue paper as I carefully placed mine under the tree on Christmas morning.

Our tree was never put up until Christmas Eve. We children hung our stockings on nails on the dining room window frame, inserted our notes to Santa, went to bed and slept after much excited giggling.

The fresh cut tree filled one corner of the front room. When we got downstairs on Christmas morning, it stood bedecked in ropes of cranberries and popcorn, a few delicate glass baubles, and clamped-on 5" candle holders on the end of each branch.

The aroma of baking pies, roasting turkey, and fresh fruit in our Christmas stockings filled our senses so that Mother nearly lost the battle to get some creamy oatmeal and hot cocoa into us on Christmas morning. The contents of our stockings were usually identical, but each item was compared one by one by each of us. We received an orange, apple, banana, nuts, hard candies or dates. A new toothbrush or comb was a standard stocking stuffer. If Santa could afford it, he would also place a tiny celluloid Kewpy doll into the very top with the fruit and peppermint sticks.

After the stocking ceremony, Mother bundled us into our matching outfits and sent us out to visit with friends so that we could show off presents. Dad took this rare day off from his work and slept until noon. Gail, my sister, and Cy, my brothers remained behind in the kitchen to help Mother get ready for dinner. Once his chores were done, Cy went out to see his boyfriends' new toys. Some might even have a sled or a coaster wagon.

We did not have out tree ceremony until after dinner was over. All of our friends had their trees on Christmas Eve or Morning.

While we little ones took a nap, Dad would get up and prepare a mystery for us. Dad also would go out rounding up aunts and uncles needing a ride. While everyone was gathering at our house, we became aware of whisperings and rustling of tissue paper. We heard this coming from the front room as each guest entered the front door.

We were much relieved when the last guest arrived because dinner was served soon after. We helped hurry the clearing of the table for pie, whipped cream and coffee for the adults. In fact, my sister and I whisked away Uncle Scott's pie plate while his last forkful was in mid-air.

Our agony was further prolong while the men enjoyed the ritual of fresh cigars. Some of the aunts helped Mother and Gail in the kitchen. The rest of us listened to Lionel Barrymore's 'Scrooge' on our metal, two-piece Atwater Kent radio in the dining room. Charles Dickens "A Christmas Carol" became a family tradition.

During this time, our great-great aunt would disappear. No sooner was "A Christmas Carol" concluded than a strange voice was heard. At first, we thought it came from the radio and then realize it came from the floor register. Next, a dim jingle of bells came from overhead and the voice at our feet told us something wonderful was about to happen. Then, we would be ushered into the front room and more jingling came and then a laden Santa came down the stairs. Santa pulled package after package form the bag and placed each one under the candle-lit tree on a snowy bed sheet.

Invariably, we received a candied fruit tray from Aunt Elizabeth in Wyoming. Traditional gifts were toothpaste, bath soaps, bath crystals, socks,. mittens, gloves, scarves, paint boxes, aprons, flannelly night wear and knit hats. Toys were a rarity. My twin sister and I received our very first dolls when we were twelve years old.

The fact that we did not have a toy to show friends took nothing away from the wonders of the holiday. Each gift or activity was enfused with imagination and enthusiasm. Love filled every corner of our house and our hearts.

I remember one year Uncle Curtis had a paying job. He splurged on Christmas gifts for my sister and me. He gave us a tiny piano. It sat on three elegant legs and made the sweetest tinkling sound when played. He also gave each of us an aquamarine silk, essayer lace trimmed hanky.

After each gift was examined and approved by everyone, the tree candles were extinguished and the wrapping tissue was carefully folded for future use. Then, we gathered around the piano and caroled by singing favorites of "Silent Night, "O Little Town of Bethlehem, and "Jingle Bells."

We had a light supper of leftovers and then Dad went out to crank the engines and clear the windshields of the frigid cars. If there was room enough, we would bundle up to keep him company on the return trip from delivering relatives home. I remember fanciful designs on the heavily, frosted car windows as we passed a street light or wreath-lighted window. As we listened to the crunch of the narrow-tired wheels on the snow covered streets, we sucked sticks of clove or peppermint candy. We also loved little filled raspberry candies and ribbon candy. The ribbon candy caused syrupy rivers to run down our chins.

New Years Day:

New Years Day rounded off the winter holiday season. Our family might go to Grandma's for an early supper. We enjoyed eating at her oilcloth-covered kitchen table while the adults sat at folding tables in other room. Other times, Aunt Fanny would invite us all to her house to sit around her beautiful mahogany table to sip oyster stew.

Then, still other times, Daddy might take us to a restaurant. The least adventurous of us would have oyster stew rather than risk the highly seasoned chili which was the specialty of the house. We kids had great fun floating little oyster crackers on our stew. In fact my memory tells me we spent more time watching our crackers sail in their creamy sea than we did eating.

The lean years brought out Mother's creativity in preparing low-cost, nutritious meals. Beans were a staple and was served in a variety of recipes. Other staples were macaroni and rice. This starchy died did not make us fat.

In fact, we were so thin that our teacher marched us to the cafeteria each school day and fed us graham crackers and milk during mid-morning. Even though we felt singled out and embarrassed, we enjoyed every last cracker and sip of milk.

My point is that holiday meals and treats of root beer or a chocolate ice cream cone were very much the exception to our lives.

Summer:

During long hot summer nights, Dad would set aside his work for an hour, put us all in the car dressed in our pajamas, and take us for a cooling ride along quiet, country roads. The breeze would soon serve as a sedative and we would doze off while Mother and Dad talked quietly of the day. Sometimes, Dad would catch us unawares by suddenly speeding along a dark road and over a deep dip. Out stomachs would leap and we would squeal in surprised shock. Dad would holler back at us, "I wish you kids would sit still back there. See what you made me do!"

Across the street from the school was a block-square wooded park. In a cleared area, there were push merry-go-rounds, swings, monkey chains, teeter-totters, and a slippery slide. Some days we would get an early start to school and we would walk through the park and play until the first bell rang. There were times when we would even dare to play for a few minutes after school even though we had strict orders to go straight home. I remember one day when my brother Cy was attacked by hornets he had disturbed. His head and eyes were painfully swollen for days.

Winter:

In the winter, our goal was to get to school and back home in the shortest possible time. There were many afternoons when we stood at the kitchen sink with tears running down our red cheeks. We were frozen and water ran over our icy fingers in a gradual thawing process. Then, Mother would apply 'Italian Balm' lotion to soother our chapped hands.

Each morning, we girls dressed in long underwear, panty waists, and garters to hold up our cotton lisle stockings. The art of lapping and holding the underwear around our ankles while pulling the long stockings up our legs was never learned by us. Mother was the only one who seemed to have mastery over this job. When we did it ourselves, we would wind up with lumpy legs.

Winter was one long-lasting world of white. Sub-zero temperatures often meant snow accumulated on the ground for weeks at a time. Driving winds built formidable drifts that would stop everything and close schools for a day or two in the city. In the country, these storms stranded livestock without food until farmers could plow through to them or airplanes could drop feed to the drifted fields.

Blizzards paralyzed all activity. No one with any sense would venture into a world where every landmark was erased. By late fall, farmers ran should high rope lines from their back doors to their barns so they could do their chores and milk the cows without getting lost in the winter blizzards.

Sometimes, a normal snow would suddenly turn into a wind-driven, raging blizzard. It would catch people away from shelter as happened to Jean and me one day.

We had walked about two blocks from school when suddenly the pretty snowflakes began swirling in an intense wind. Immediately, we could not see a tree or a house. We luckily stumbled into a garage that had been left open. After the storm abated enough, Dad got out in his car to look for us. He found us huddled and shivering in the garage. We cried and shook all the way home. When we arrived there, mother peeled us out of our wet clothes, wrapped each of us in a cotton flannel sheet, and put us to bed. Dad's silence and getting no supper told us more than a thousand, scolding words of the risks we had taken by leaving school that day.

On rare occasions, Mother would drive us to school. These times were when the morning temperature was too cold and was dangerous or if there was a driving rain storm. I remember the funny little rubber-bladed defroster fan mounted near the windshield. Eventually, it would thaw a patch of thick ice just large enough for Mother to peer through as she drove the big Buick car.

Spring:

On the first day of Spring, we would unfasten our garters, roll down our stockings to our ankles, and roll up the underwear above our knees as soon as we were out of Mother's sight. We did not mind coats, hats, scarves, mitten and galoshes as much as we disliked the long underwear. Our red chapped knees gave us away because freezing Nebraska winters do not end simply because of a date on the calendar. In fact, a May snow storm was not unheard of.

Teenage Years:

The Depression had its greatest imp[act on my sister and I during our Junior High School years. It was during this time there was not enough money for us to continue to dress alike. Instead, we had to wear hand-me-downs from our cousins, Mary Sims and Kathleen Russell. We felt we were very poor and it was more than clear to our schoolmates. We were very self-conscious this and felt we were wearing signboards advertising the fact.

Our early teen years were torture enough without this additional embarrassment. We were growing so that that we were taller than most of the boys and all of the girls at the junior high. We were also painfully thin and appeared to be all arms, legs and necks. People began calling us "Toothpick" and we hated it as it haunted us. Our self-awareness reached such an extreme that we tried not to walk together so as not to be so noticeable by passersby. Our identical twinness was a burden for a few years. It was especially bad when we had to leave school in the middle of the day because we began menstruating and our dresses were stained.

My sister and I seemed to exude an aura of vulnerability that attracted tough kids. They loved to pick on us all the way home from school. The badgering continued for several weeks until an acquaintance named Leah decided to be our bodyguard.

Leah was a powerfully, muscled Negro girl with whom we shared gym class and where she excelled. She was obviously as poor as we were, but she had all the self-assurance we lacked.

When the bell rang at the end of school, Leah accompanied us past the gauntlet of our tormentors. After just one confrontation with Leah, the threat from these toughs fizzled out like a punctured balloon. By the end of the year, our brave shadow had weaned us from her protective surveillance.

During high school, Jean and I became acquainted with other Negro classmates. The Negro population in Lincoln represented less than one percent of the total population. They lived for the most part in an area north of downtown. This area bordered the University of Nebraska campus.

There was an active chapter of the Urban League. There was no separation in theaters or other social gathering places. However, opportunity in work places was probably no better in Lincoln, Nebraska than it was in Lincolnton, North Carolina in the 1930's. Negro were servants, Pullman porters, janitors, etc. There were no separate public restrooms or schools, but their religious worship was in separate churches and this was by choice, I believe.

The few Negro students at Lincoln High took pride in scholastic excellence. One of the boys lettered in scholastics and sports. He was tremendously popular for his personality and integrity.

Entertainment:

We had an Atwater Kent radio. It had static, squeals and fading volumes that frustrated the avid listeners of the family. As the industry grew, reception improved and we became fans of the early radio stars. There was Ed Wynne, Eddie Cantor, Joe E. Brown and Kate Smith. Programming included 'play-by play' baseball games, poetry reading by Edgar Guest, music by large orchestras, and rich voices artists such as Lawrence Tibbet. Gail turned into broadcasts of the Metropolitan Opera and I had a crush on an Irish balladeer who had a regular weekday afternoon program. The ladies of the family listened to "My Gal Sunday," "Ma Perkins," "Helen Trent", "Stella Dallas", and other soap operas while we sewed or rested on a hot, summer afternoon.

We also enjoyed "Easy Aces" with Vic and Sadie, "Fibber Magee and Molly", Lum 'N Abner" at their Jotem Down Store, "Jimmy Allen," "Jack Armstrong, the All American Boy," "I love a Mystery, "The Shadow," and "One Man's Family." Thanks to radio many entertainers gained national followings. Some of them were Bing Crosby, Fre Allen, Ben Bernie, Bob Hop[e, Edgar Bergen and Charlie McCarthy, George Burns and Gracie Allen, and Jack Benny and Mary Livingston.

We also had favorite mellow-voiced announcers. These included Ben Grauer, Don Wilson, Harry Vonselle, and Don and Jim Ameche.

Eight-by-ten glossies of movie stars of the 1920's and 1930's were the precursor to World War II pin-up pictures that GI's taped to their locker door or carried into battle with them. Mother and Gail had pictured on their bedroom walls of Clara Bow, Janet Gaynor, Delores Del Rio, Colleen Moore, Jean Harlow and other glamour queens of the day.

We twins were allowed to walk to the downtown theaters with Gail and Cy for Saturday morning nickel or dime adventure moves. Tom Mix and Buck Jones were the most popular cowboy stars, but I fell in love with Tim McCoy. Rin Tin Tin, the move star German Shepherd dog, was very popular and had his own feature films. Serials, often referred to as "Cliff Hangers," kept us filled with anticipation from one Saturday to the next.

Jean and I shared a pair of roller skates and matching skinned knees by falling on the uneven sidewalk. We treasured our skates and were torment to have to wait for our turn. Mother got exasperated and made us each use one skate. The lucky one got the left skate because it was easier to push off with the right foot.

Another typical diversion during the summer was walking on large tin cans. The trick was to find a pair of large cans which had been drained by punching a hole in each end. With our feet protected by shoes, we jounced on the side of each can until they formed snug- fitting appendages. (These were the original elevator shoes). The foot gear was noisy and was worn on sidewalks to get the best effect. They were taboo indoors.

We also entertained ourselves with "Big Little Books." They were four-inch cubs sold at the dime store and featured fascinating adventures of comic strip heroes, such as Tarzan, Tailspin Tommy, Dick Tracy, and Little Orphan Annie. We swapped these with our friends and was the forerunner of trading comic books for a future generation.

The "Bobsey Twins" books were naturally favorites of ours. We fell in love with "Alice in Wonderland", Tweedle Dee and Tweedle Dum," and "Nancy Drew."

Jacks, marbles, and jumping rope were favorite activities. The boys sniffed at the idea of any girls who thought they should be allowed to shoot a game of marble with them. After all, they were the experts!

Jumping rope wore off a lot of shoe leather so Depression-pressed parents dreaded to see the season arrive knowing their children, especially the girls, would be skipping rope from morning to evening. "Hop-Scotch" also wore off a lot of leather and was enjoyed by boys and girls. Skipping, hopping, scooting across the squares while picking up the game store and tossing it on the last space without losing your balance was the goal.

Another game we played was "Fox and Geese." This holds a special place in our memories because our Dad took time away from work to introduce us to it. Dad started by tramping out a hug circle in the snow and adding spokes to form a big wheel. We followed in his big footsteps to help him lay the foundation for the game. Then, Dad took the part of the "Fox" and we were the "Geese." The goal was for the geese to escape capture by the fox without steeping out of the wheel rim or spokes. A captured goose was out of the game. The last goose captured got to be the fox in the next game. The hub was the safety zone and no goose could be captured while they were there, but there was a time limit, and another goose could chase the first one out of the hub while feeling the fox.

After the excitement of this game, we would make snow angels by lying down on our back and swinging our arms full length through the snow. The blue sky glittered overhead, the world was muffled in silence, and we would carefully get up, climb the terrace, and look down to admire our angels.

Mother taught us care games. She also had a special card shuffle. Fan-Tan was known as "Seven Up." The object was to play in turn around the table building up or down on the sevens of each suit as they were played in the center of the table. One player won by playing his last card first.

We also enjoyed "Slap Jack." The aim here was to be the first to slap a Jack as cards were played face up forming a stock. The successful players wound up with the most cards after the last Jack had been played and slapped.

Another indoor activity was The Scrap Book. Mother kept this large album in her cedar chests, which signified its specialness. We collected magazine pictures, Valentines, and other illustrated materials we felt were worthy of a place in The Scrap Book.

On bad-weather days or when we were recuperating form illness, Mother unlocked the cedar chest and carried the book to the dining table. We would gather around and look over the books carefully before settling down to decide what new candidates would qualify to be added to The Book. Pictures of angels, Campbell Soup kids, Cupids, pretty ladies, an RCA Victor ad, Buster Brown, or a Firestone ad of a yawning boy in his Doctor Denton pajamas with a light candle would win places in the scrap book.

As teenagers, we loved to spend warm evenings playing ball in the street after doing the supper dishes. However, if there was one speck of food on any dish, Dad would make us leave our game and do every dish over again - washing, drying, and putting every dish, pot, pan, glass and flatware away. I remember this as torture!

My brother, Cy, made wonderful things when Dad gave him time off from helping with car repair jobs. He made wooden guns that fired bands cut from old inner tubes, sling shots, and a soapbox car. Orange crates made up the body of the car and the wheels were scrounged from junk piles. Rope was attached to the axles and operated by a rough steering wheel. The car was painted with leftover paint, and we girls were so impressed we begged to test drive it.

Cy also made a pair of stilts that increased his heights so that his head seemed to brush the clouds. He finally put the stilts away during the summer he grew to be 6 feet-7 1/2 inches.

Cy also had a bullet-making set. He melted chunks of lead in a heavy ladle over the gas flame on Mother's stove and poured the molten lead into heavy molds to cool.

We played quiet games as well. On rainy days or when we were at our great aunts' house, we would play "Button, Button, Who's Got the Button," and "Hide the Thimble". This game was where the seekers were advised they we getting 'hot' or 'cold' depending on how near they were to the object.

"Pussy Wants A Corner" was a porch game we played during rainy weather. "Pussy" tried to catch the other players off guard by dashing into one of their corners while they tried to swap an opposite corner with a playmate. It took five children to play this game. There was one child for each corner and one who was the "Pussy" The "Pussy" had to meow and whine, "Pussy wants a corner," until he or she gained a corner.'

Our duplicate was only three blocks away from a large field adjoining the railroad yards and Gooch's Mill. Each spring, the circus came to town and set up in this field. The free entertainment afforded by watching the caravan make its way down A street excited us beyond containment. We were enthralled with the daisy chain of silently plodding elephants, with one elephant holding the tail of the one in front of him, the artfully decorated red wagons, the strutting, waving acrobats, and the capering clowns.

We begged to Mother until she allowed Cy to take us to the ground so we could watch the roustabouts erect the huge tents. Later one night, we even got to watch the dismantling process. I remember the growls, groans, and stench of the men and the animals very well. Once, we were taken to see the show under the "Big Top" and ate cotton candy. The anticipation was almost unbearable, and we drove our parents crazy by asking, "It is time to go yet?" endlessly.

One of our neighbors were the Dietermeyers. Mr. Dietermeyer worked at Miller & Paine Department Store. He was one of the few white collar workers in our neighborhood. He left like clock work each morning and returned punctually each evening. He always wore a dark serge suit, stiffly collard white shirt, and a dark tie. He walked past our house to the streetcar two blocks away. He frequently walked the entire 36 blocks to and from work when the water was mile to save on car fare.

Mrs. Dietermeyer was a large, rusty-haired woman. She bustled about her daily tasks caring for three daughters and three sons. She kept an immaculate home and baked all of their bread, roots, cakes, pies, cookies, and doughnuts. She made soap for the family wash and supervised the tending of the chickens and garden behind the house in the middle of our blocks.

My mother and Mrs. Dietermeyer wages a competition each wash day. They tried to have the cleanest, whitest, brightest wash on their lines.

Like most of the mothers, Mrs. Dietermeyer did not allow the children to play inside her house. I do recall one time being in her basement and smelling the smothering kettle of lye and naphtha bubbling in a heavy, black, iron soap kettle.

Streetcars operated in Lincoln until the late 1930's. Buses took over as public transportation after that. We rarely rode either unless the weather was too severe to walk to town on an errand. I even walked a 30 block round tip while under treatment for planter wards on the bottom of my feet!"

- JMW (excerpt from <u>Nip and Tuck</u>) - Nebraska

.   .   .

"My most vivid memory was we did not have money to buy things.

95

I remember hoboes coming to the door at the farm. Mother always fed them and sent them on their way and Dad found them sleeping in our barns. Hoboes were not bad people, but mama did not want us to get too friendly.

We lost our only son to pneumonia when he was a year old. The funeral was small and simple. We never had another son - only daughters after that.

At Halloween, the kids would go door-to-door. They got popcorn, apples, and cookies. They usually wore their regular clothes with masks. Favorite tricks were to soap windows uptown or tip over outhouses.

During Christmas, the adults did not get gifts. They saved their money for the children. Times were hard and the children only received one gift, like a doll.

Our clothes were hand-me-downs or homemade. I remade clothes for my daughters from my own old, middy blouses. Underwear was made from flour sacks and cute dresses from feed sacks. Our wardrobes were two outfits per person. We had one to wear and one to wash.

Everybody was in the same boat during the Depression and we did not think much about it."

- Nebraska

.   .   .

"Most of our clothes were homemade during the Depression. I recall one of my friend's mother would use old inner tubes to make elastic for undergarments so that they would hold up when you wore them. She would take an inner tube and cut it a very fine length in order to do this."

- Texas

.   .   .

"I grew up in Aberdeen, South Dakota. I was the oldest of five children, three sisters and one brother. I was age 13 when the Depression years began in 1930.

My father was a chemistry professor and worked as Head of the Physical Science Department at Northern State College. Although my father was employed in the 1930's, I do recall he took a cut in pay during this period of time.

In 1928, my father bought a 1917 open touring Ford. It had isinglass windows that snapped in place. This car was used only for special occasions like Sunday drives and visits to the family.

Our house was about a mile from the college. My father would walk to work in the morning, walk home for lunch, and then walk back home at night in all kinds of weather. I recall our winters were 40 degrees below zero and our summers were 115 degrees in the shade.

My father's office was on the top floor of a three and one-half story building with no elevator. His mail was not delivered to him and he had to walk up and down the stairs and several blocks on the campus in order to get his mail.

Our closest relations were from my mother's family. They lived in Monticello, Minnesota. This was 280 miles from where we lived. My father was busy at work all year except for the month of August. During this month, we traveled to see my mother's family and often would travel by train.

When we visited family, it was a two day trip to Minnesota. About 100 miles into the trip, we would stop and rent a cabin. It was strictly a cabin. You had to go down the street to go to the bathroom. There was a ten mile stretch of road on the way to our relatives that was a dirt road. I recall one time when it rained on our trip. We drove sideways during the entire time on that strip of road!

My mother was a frugal cook. We ate lots of spaghetti, macaroni and cheese, and cornmeal. She was famous for her chicken dinners on Sunday with lots of mashed potatoes, noodles, or dumplings. There were also times when she went to the butcher and got "mock" chicken legs. These legs were made of veal and were very economical.

For birthdays, we had cake. On July Fourth, we enjoyed fireworks. Christmas was the happiest holiday. I usually got books and our New York members of the family would send dresses to my sisters.

I remember terrible dust storms in the 1930's. You could actually taste the grit and dirt that got into your mouth when you talked. There was so much wind and dust blowing that the tumbleweeds would get lodged in the fences. Then, the dirt and silt would get caught and cover up the fence, and then, the animals would simply walk over them and get lost.

After I finished high school, I started school at the teacher's college. Later, I went to Rapid City, South Dakota to the School of Mines to get my engineering degree. I had dining hall privileges during the week at school, but not on the weekends. There were many times when my Sunday dinner was a ten-cent candy bar. In 1937-38, I worked as an assistant to the chemistry professor. I did lab work and graded papers.

I finished school in January of 1939, but my official graduation was not until June. During this time, I worked at a natural gas distributor. I recall being paid about $100 a month. (Graduates were paid $125.)

As a personal note, Mount Rushmore was started before the Depression and work did not stop until World War II began. I recall the original plan was to have the figures go down to the waist. Many South Dakota people sighed with a great deal of relief when the work finally stopped.

There was also one time when our church decided to provide relief to a family with desperate needs on our block. The church gathered food and other staples and went to the house. When the lady of the house realized who they were and the purpose of the visit, she slammed her door shut and refused the help."

- JHJ - South Dakota

.   .   .

"I grew up around Beaver City, Oklahoma. This area is in the panhandle of the sate and is often referred to as No Man's Land or the Great Dust Bowl.

Our area was desolate and poor. All we knew were dust storms. The dust came in big, dark, black clouds. Fence poles blew up in the air and the clouds were so dark and black we had to turn our kerosene lamps on in the middle of the day. We used cotton masks over our faces and dampened blankets and burlap at the windows to try to keep the dust out, but there was so much dust being blown it came through cracks in our houses we did not know we even had.

The book, 'The Grapes of Wrath,' did not really tell all the story of what our area was really like. The rich and wealthy people, who owned two mattress, were the ones of us who packed up and moved on to California during the Depression. Those of us who were really poor stayed behind and struggled.

I grew up with no immediate family or relatives around. I was the middle one of three boys. My father was a mailman and farmed a 160-acre farm.

We grew everything we needed. We had lots of chickens. Even much later in life, my mother would offer us nothing but fried chicken when we visited. Chicken continued to be a special meal for her.

We had a root cellar and no refrigeration. We canned many of our meats with a pressure cooker. When we butchered beef or pork, our family pooled together with neighbors and shared the meat or else it would spoil. We picked wild plums and had lots of plum butter and plum jelly to eat. When we killed chickens, my brothers and I would develop an assembly line to kill, pluck, and cook them.

I recall we grew tomatoes in our garden, and had lots of chicken, gravy and biscuits for our meals. We drank milk from our own cows and took turns from year to year raising animals to butcher for the four families that shared. That meant every fourth or fifth year we were responsible for feeding and caring for these animals until we butchered them.

We had very few celebrations in our family. Christmas might bring an orange and a toy truck.

Our real celebration was after the wheat harvest. We would make ice cream and play baseball while our parents played cards. This took place in cottonwood trees by the creek.

Our area did not have many trees. We used very cheap coal and cow chips for heat. Kerosene was used for lighting and cooking.

I remember I did most of the housework and we took care of ourselves when we were ill. We were really country folk and were very much on our own.

We walked three miles to our school. Sometimes we rode a horse, and in bad weather, my father would walk us part way to school. By the time, I went to high school, we had a bus. It would leave at 7:00 a.m. and we would get home at 5:30 p.m. It was a long day. In the winter, we would leave in the dark and come home in the dark.

I was happy to have something to eat. I do not recall anything I did not like while I was growing up.

I had no sweetheart in school. Instead, I was more interested in good grades and getting a good education. I was more interested in making sure I did not grow up to live on a farm. I did not like farm work and knew I wanted to be a bookkeeper, accountant and auditor. Because of this, I concentrated on excelling in math at school.

On Fridays at school, we would have math contests. We chose sides and competed on who could add, subtract, multiply, and divide the best. I found myself on the winning side most of the time.

I recall my idol was a man at the local store. He could take three columns of numbers and add them all up at the same time. This fascinated me and I wanted my father to trade with him so that I could watch him work.

My father disliked FDR. It had taken our family many years to build up our hear to 20 cattle. Because farm prices were so depressed, FDR passed a law where you were only allowed so many farm animals. The inspectors came. Our allotment was six cattle and 14 of our cattle were skilled. My father felt bitter about this because he felt FDR had put him in a position where he had to beg. My father was a proud man and did not want to beg from anyone. It was a real struggle for our family to make it and he felt FDR's fireside chats were a way of making fun of the poor people. He also felt the rules were not fair because some people traded their cattle and were not touched by this law.

In the 1960's, my family moved to Ohio. I was fascinated by all the trees. When our first fall came, we felt the woods were on fire from all the bright reds we saw on those wonderful trees."

- HR - Oklahoma

.   .   .

"My grandfather left Kansas and was one of the participants in the 1889 "Run" in the Oklahoma territory. This "Run" was used to settle the opened territory and people staked out claims on 160-acres plots of land. He claimed land outside of Clinton, Oklahoma. The original farm is still in our family and I have bricks from the farm house stamped O.T. (Oklahoma Territory). The original house still stands, but is now used for feed storage and hay.

I recall the dust storms were very bad in the 1930's. I used to go around with a wet rag across my face so that I could breathe. Dust to this day still bothers me.

My mother's family was Russian and my father's family was German. I was fortunate to be part of a large and close family group. Our family consisted of three brothers who married three sisters.

Our family were Mennonites. Ladies could not cut their hair and the pews were separated where the men sat on one side of the church and the ladies sat on the other side.

Our family was very active in our church. My grandfather donated the land for the church and the cemetery. My father was the Sunday School superintendent and also the choir director.

Every second Sunday we had Christian endeavor. It was a day of celebration and we had party games in the afternoon. On Sundays, we always had banana pies, good, and my mother made a yeast dressing with raisins or plums to stuff in and around the goose.

Our family was very big and close. The children had to wait for their meals. The men ate first, then the women, and then the boys. The girls always ate last, and by that time, the banana pie was usually gone.

On Saturday, my mother prepared the Sunday meal. The house had to be sparkling clean for Sunday, too. We had to polish all the shows. Our silver was tin and the knives rusted easily. It was my job to clean the silver.

Breakfast always started with devotion. We also had a memory card we had to memorize each Sunday.

At Christmas, we always had a special program to memorize. We also celebrated two holidays at each of our grandparents' houses. We did not receive lots of gifts. The girls would get rag dolls made by our mothers. Then, we would get new clothes for our dolls in the years afterwards.

We had a large garden and raised most of our own food. The root cellars was always full with canned goods. We raised turkeys, ducks and chickens. We also separated the milk. Our parents would go into town once a week and sell ten gallons of cream and a gross of eggs. They got eight cents a dozen for their eggs. Our hens sat on their brood of eggs until they hatched. Our wheat went to the mill to be ground for flour.

The girls' dressed and underwear were made from flour sacks. My mother also made dish towels from the flour sacks and I still have a few of them in my home. The sacks were very beautiful with blue stripes. Our sheets were made from sugar sacks. The boys' coveralls were ordered.

Our family were all good cooks. Chocolate cake was a real special treat. We always had lots of fruit for pies. My mother also made a delicious Swiegback bread. This is a German recipe which I am trying to teach my grandchildren to make as a family tradition.

Funerals were held in the house and the bodies were hauled in a wagon. It was important to bury people as soon as possible since there was no embalming.

Each year, our family celebrated harvest time. We all rode in the back of my uncle's truck and went to the state zoo in Oklahoma City. There were six adults and 15 of us children. We celebrated with homemade ice cream, cookies, cakes, and fried chicken. We also had Neighi soda pops. Our favorite flavors were strawberry and grape.

In the summers, a Negro man would walk from Alabama to our farm in Oklahoma and stay with us. I recall he was about 50 and he did little things like babysitting and making wire egg baskets for my mother. He ate with our family and slept in the granary.

When he first showed up, my father asked him what he wanted to be called. The man replied, "Nigger Bill will be fine." (The word Nigger was not a bad or derogatory word in our language in the 1930's)

At the end of summer, Nigger Bill would return to Alabama. He came and visited with us for seven summers. We children always looked forward to his return.

I recall our county seat had a rule that Negroes were only allowed to live across the railroad tracks. They were also not allowed to come into town after sundown. Because of these rules, my parents were always careful and cautious about their relationship with Nigger Bill.

In 1938, I graduated from high school. I gave my picture to my cousin. During harvest, my brother informed us that he had had a dream our house burned down. Within an hour of telling us this, our house caught fire and burned to the ground. We lost everything. My graduation photo survived because of my cousin.

My brother continued to have these type of dreams all of his life. It occurred again when our mother died.

In the late 1930's, my cousins got jobs with the WPA and were pleased. They participated in building a Shelter Belt. This project consisted of planting seven rows of trees on farms. These trees were planted in order to keep the topsoil of the farms from being blown away."

- FR - Oklahoma

.   .   .

"I grew up in the mid-eastern part of South Dakota in "The Dirty Thirties." The 1930's were dirty because of the dust storms we had. The dust was like a blizzard and many people and animals became lost in these storms. Our fences were made of netting. The tumbleweeds would lodge in the fence and then dirt would pile up and create snowdrifts which the animals wandered over and got lost.

My parents were farmers. For a period of about seven years, we had no rain which resulted in no crops which meant we had no cash. My parents sold cream and eggs for cash and they sold cattle to pay the taxes.

The weather was very windy during this time, too. We had a saying when people asked us if it was windy in South Dakota. We would answer, "Does the sun come up in the east?"

We only had four things we had to buy. They were sugar, flour, matches and kerosene. Our flour and sugar was bought in 50-pound bags.

Our family homesteaded the farm. We all worked together to keep from losing it. My mother stressed to us the important of keeping the farm. This farm is still in the family and is now a Century Farm with us as the same family owning it for 100 years. It is still very important to us, and when we speak of it, it is "THE FARM" in big, capital letters.

I was in the eighth grade when the Depression started. We were poor, but did not know it. We used everything and sometimes the same thing was used over and over again. Recycling for us was an everyday event. My mother made me a skirt from my father's wedding trousers. I did not have a bought coat until I was thirteen years old. Our water was first used to wash clothes. Then, we would use the same water to wash the porch and finally the same water was used to water my mother's much cherished cut-leaf weeping birch. The tree did not survive the weather.

Sewing was a necessity for my mother and we knew we were never to touch her scissors - ever! She had a pair to cut cloth and a pair to cut hair. Using them was off-limits for all of us. Some of our flour sacks were fancy with flowers on them. These were made into dresses. The non-floral flour sacks were made into dish towels.

Our winters were fierce. We used layers of heavy clothing to stay warm. The Sears catalog also came in the winter. We would cut paper dolls and embroider to entertain ourselves. I remember when we ordered from the catalog it took only three days before the order arrived at our home.

We had trees on our farm. Because we had a tree claim on one-quarter of land, my grandfather purchased it for $17.

Our social life was centered around church and school. The Christmas program at church was the highlight of the year. We practiced all day on Saturdays during the month of December for this special program.

We doctored ourselves when we became ill. Kerosene and Epson salts were our cures. We only saw the dentist if we had an awful toothache and used cloves to kill the pain until we could get the tooth pulled. I recall we had whooping cough, measles, and my sister had a terrible illness with scarlet fever.

My grandparents were Norwegian. I remember my grandmothers taking wool from sheep, carding and spinning it. Then, they would knit the wool into mittens, socks, and sweaters.

At Christmas, the great event was for us to have Lute Fisk. This was codfish cured in lye and ashes. It smelled awful. Because of our cattle, all of our vegetables were creamed. We also had Lefsa.

If we passed a barn that had been painted, we knew the farm had been bought by insurance people. This was how families from our area got the money to go to California where things were better.

My grandparents had put all their money in the bank to finance their retirement. The banks closed and they lost all their money. Because of this, they were forced to live with us. Later, we also had another family live with us at times. My grandfather made willow tree baskets. Then, he would pick chokeberries and we would make jelly from them.

One year our parents told us if we helped out in the fields then maybe we could get a new winter coat. My coat was green with a fur collar.

In the late 1930's, rain finally came and we had crops again. During this time, my father would go into town and hire migrants to help in the potato fields. My father was a very kind-hearted man, but he once had to let a man go because he had gotten drunk off drinking vanilla.

My parents were Republicans. They feared and disliked the Roosevelts. My mother was convinced the NRA was a sign of the beast and the Book of Revelations was coming to pass."

- MD - South Dakota

.   .   .

"My memories of the Depression years are somewhat vague. My father was a Methodist minister assigned to the South California Conference. In those days, ministers were transferred every two or three years so I lived in more places than I can remember.

During the real Depression years, we lived in Pomona, California. At that time, Pomona was in the middle of large orange groves. The church was quite large and many families were well-off even in those times. I do not recall ever going hungry. A lot of what we ate was donated by the parishioners. The churches my father was assigned to always furnished a parsonage as housing, too. The housing was never plush, but it was always adequate."

- PHR - California

.   .   .

"I was born in 1920 at the home of my great aunt in Madison, South Dakota. I was the only girl in the family and have no doubt I received more than my share of attention from both my parents and four older brothers who loved to tease me.

My childhood years were fulfilled with the many typical experiences of farm life in the days of no running water or electricity. Care and concern for both life and material things was an accepted way of life. For my first eight years, my education was acquired in a little one room country school house.

After completion of the eight grades, my education was set aside for one year with a considerable mount of 4-H activity filling in. In the 1930's, a bus ride to school was unheard of. Carrying our lunch pail and books, we walked to and from school over woven wire fences with two to three lines of barbed wire of top. This took some skill to make sure some part of our clothing did not get caught and tear. The distance to school was about one mile via the shortcuts. It was one and a half miles if we followed the road.

On very rare occasions, my father would lift me atop old Sailor's back for a horse back ride to school. Sailor was one of the older horses and rather special. I would slide off his back at school, give Sailor a pat, and tell him to go home. He always did.

Only when the weather was bad, did Dad hook up the wagon or barnyard sleight to get us to school. Our school hours were from 9:00 a.m. to 4:00 p.m. with recesses and lunch hour for eating and games. There was no inside plumbing, and we had a community water pail and dipper for drinking. We all used the one enameled wash dish or pan and tossed the dirty water outside on the ground. Of course, we ran outside to the 'outhouses' at the rear of the school yard when necessary regardless of the weather conditions. Somehow, I think we were healthier in those days. We never worried about germs!

Our school library held perhaps 50 to 75 books. I remember one of my favorites was <u>Pinocchio.</u> Our teacher had to be able to handle any difficulty. She was janitor, coach, nurse, musician, and of course, teacher. She even hauled coal from the shed to start and keep fires going in the old, big stove on cold winter days. The stove was surrounded by a hug sheet metal casing to keep us from being burned getting near it for warmth.

September through part of May were regular school months. Then, we had a month of Parochial School in June at another school two miles southeast of the farm. Our transportation there was usually by horse and single buggy. Parochial School was much like the present day Vacation Bible School, but it was structured more on regular school guidelines with classes in memory, history, and spelling on Biblical subjects.

Being five years younger than my youngest brother, I grew up helping mother with the many chores. My four brothers were needed in the fields. However, Marvin, the youngest, was very adept in assisting with household chores including ironing dress shirts.

Mother loved plants and flowers so the yard encircling our house was an array of pleasant color during the spring and summer months. We planted a huge vegetable garden every year. The 1930's were dry years and much water had to be carried to sustain growth in the garden.

We had two cisterns for drinking, bathing, and washing. The well water was not good but was pumped into tanks for the cattle and the horses. Some homes were equipped with inside kitchen pumps, but ours was not so we carried water in large galvanized buckets. The kitchen range was equipped with a side 'reservoir' that kept water warm for bathing and other uses. A large tea-kettle always sat ready on the stove and ready to boil for a quick cup of tea.

The 'dinner' hour was always at noontime and all the men looked forward to a big meal. There were many times a forenoon lunch was taken out the field workers, but always an afternoon lunch of sandwiches, cake, cookies, and coffee which gave the men a restful break.

The evening meal was 'supper' and consisted of a much lighter meal. There were perhaps cold potatoes, home prepared cold cuts, bread and butter, and usually topped of with a slice or two of cream and bread with fruit sauce (home canned) on top. During those lean years, we sold our cream, and I recall Mother purchasing Oleo margarine. It was white with a capsule of yellow food coloring included. We had to break the capsule and work in the color to make it look like butter. Naturally, we preferred the home churned butter.

All this required a lot of preparation, including harvesting much from the garden, and sitting in the shade hulling the peas, snapping beans, and peeling potatoes. And, Boy! could the flies bite!

On many summer days, the temperature was 104 degrees in the shade. I remember Mother laying wet towels over her shoulders as she baked 18 large loaves of bread every other day! Bread seemed to the main stay for the hard working men.

We also did our own butchering of beef, pork, and lamb. This had to be done during the coldest part of winter so that the meat could be stored in a closed-off room where it would stay very cold until all the parts could be cut up, and cured or canned. Mother had a technique of oven canning that turned out wonderfully delicious. For meat balls, we kids helped by running the meat pieces through an old fashioned hand grinder.

Springtime was perhaps the most delightful time of the year. I remember the wonderful fragrance of lilacs, fresh lettuce leaves and radishes from Mom's 'hot bed' garden, the fun of checking the little sandy knoll on the southwest end of our land for the Pasque flowers (the South Dakota flower) which was better known to us as the Mayflower. The yellow buttercup blossomed here also. In a ditch along the road on the south edge of the farm was a cluster of pussy willow shrubs. I loved the feel of the soft furry tufts on each branch.

One of my Dad's hobbies was raising gorgeous Peonies of all varieties. These came in full bloom during the month of June. People came for miles to see and purchase a dozen or so blossom for 25 cents or have Dad take orders for roots to be supplied in September at dividing time. One one occasion, I cut an armload of blossoms for some strangers from Madison. In using my Daddy's jack knife, I accidentally slipped on a stem and jabbed the blade into o my just below the knee cap. I still have the scar to this day.

I also recall the Ladies Aid sponsoring an Ice Cream Social at the farm for everyone to view the Peonies. We also had festivities of pie, cake, ice cream, coffee, AND Soda Pop (all flavors) for five cents a bottle! This was special for us kids as we seldom saw or tasted the sweet delight!

On Fourth of July, we always looked forward to a super dinner of new potatoes, creamed fresh peas, fried spring chicken, water melon (which we called 'green pig'), and lemonade. The chickens we raised. We hatched them in our incubator and purchased them from a wholesaler by the hundred count.

We also raised turkeys and geese. We also had a couple of Guinea hens that always seemed to say 'Joe Clap.' Of course, there was the usual horses, milking cows, steers, calves, pigs and sheep. The steers, pigs, and sheep were a source of added income, and Dad would haul a load of pigs in a truck to Sioux Falls when he felt he could get a good price. I remember many times when we would bring in an orphaned pig or lamb, wrap it in an old piece of blanket, keep it near the kitchen stove for warmth, and feed it from the bottle. Special bottle nipples were always on hand for these emergencies.

Our main source of income was from the sales of grains. We raised primarily oats, barley, wheat, corn, and alfalfa. Much of this was stored for food for the animals and harvest time came in late July and August. The women spent weeks in preparation to feed all the extra help during the three to four days of threshing. The men in the neighborhood shared the work as each farm owner took his turn to have his grain threshed.

Some of the summer days were spent snaring gophers with a piece of string at the top of the gopher hole. We would lay flat on our stomachs and whistle what we thought was a coaxing sound to a gopher. It usually worked and soon the gopher would come out to check out the area. If one was quick enough, a fast yank might catch the rascal. I will never forget one day when I spied one in our front yard. I ran into the ice house to pick up my brother's rifle and aimed it at the gopher standing up high and cocky. It was hard for me to believe but I made a direct hit and that was the last of that gopher.

The Ice House was a small building my Dad had built over a 15 foot deep ten by ten square hole in the ground. It had a built in stair to the bottom. In the winter, this hole would be filled with ice blocks hauled in from Lake Campbell. This supplied our refrigeration in the summer months. The ground gradually absorbed the slow melting ice. It was a bit dangerous, especially toward the end of the summer. One time, I slipped and fell 15 feet in late summer. I came up with only a few bruises, but I was crying hard because I had broken Mother's butter dish.

There was always much to do on the farm. We harvested fruit from the orchard. I hated sitting in the Choke Cherry tree and picking those tiny cherries. We also had garden vegetables to tend, picking up corn cobs in the pig pen for kindling, feeding the chickens and picking the eggs, bottle feeding lambs, carrying water, washing the separator and milk pails, and our evenings were spent hoeing weeds until the mosquitoes chased us inside.

How my Mother found time for all her handiwork projects I will never know. She sewed my clothes, washed, ironed with flat irons, knitted, crocheted, tatted, did bead work, and made rugs from torn strips of old material that she sewed together on an old treadle machine and rolled these strips into balls to be crocheted into rugs later. She also made many piece quilts. I remember many times that her home-made quilt frame rested on four dining room chairs set up in the parlor while she did the quilting whenever she could find a spare minute during the daylight hours.

Our only night time light was by kerosene lamps. The brightest light was from an Aladdin lamp in the center of the dining room table. This was where we did our homework or played a game of dominoes with the family. Our kitchen light was a lamp that fit into a bracket attached to the wall high above. It was near the cooking range or stove. I am now the proud possessor of this lamp and it is attached to my breakfast nook wall.

Washing clothes was not easy. The water had to be heated on the stove in a large copper boiler. The usually very solid clothes were soaked in the tubs the night before. In the summertime, we could be outside near the cistern, but in the winter, it was all crowded into the small kitchen. The old hand wash board was used for only small jobs. Up until the introduction of FelsNaphta and other soap powders, Mother made her own soap for clothing washing with tallow and lye.

We had acquired a wash machine that could activate the agitator by pumping a handle back and forth. I vividly recall being set to the task of pumping many times. During this time, I was advised it was also a good time to study my lesson for Saturday catechism class. The clothes were put through a hand wringer, rinsed in a tub of cool water, and wrung again. Then, we hung them on outdoor lines to sun and dry.

In the wintertime, I remember our long underwear was stiff as a board. We would bring them in and drape them over string lines in the house near the heater. We had a wood burning stove in the dining room and a big charcoal heater in the parlor.

Our upstairs received no heat unless a little bit slipped through the cracks. There were many mornings I would awake to view the neat paintings of Jack Frost on my window in the winter. We often made a hurried dash down the stairs to finish dressing in front to the oven door in the kitchen.

We grew up with the understanding that bathing was a weekly affair. During the winter months, the kitchen was the bathroom after all the Saturday chores were done. Heat from the cook stove oven kept things cozy as we dipped warm water from the reservoir into the family wood tub, which was approximately 30 inches in diameter. Remember... we only had outhouses for toilets, no running water, and no bathtubs! Running through the snow to the outhouse at night was not much fun. Especially, when you had to be sure, you didn't run into the clothes line on the way. Thank goodness for moon lit nights!

We did have a big Turkey Dinner with all the extras on Thanksgiving. Brother Marvin was a real pro at sticking and de-feathering his turkeys for market and one for us.

Christmas Eve was always a meal of Lute Fisk, Lefse, and Sweet Soup. Usually, Dad had arrived home with a nice tree that the lumber yard in Volga had given him. Old favorite decorations were added. After all the dishes were done, everyone gathered in the parlor to light the candles that were clipped on the tree. We watched quietly while the candles burned as far as we dared let them.

Gift giving was not a major part of our Christmas. If there were some gifts around the three, they were opened and enjoyed. On Christmas day, there was usually a church service to attend. Then, we would return home to enjoy a roast goose dinner. Mom had prepared some geese for market and kept one for our dinner. What a job it was to dip the goose in hot water and then hurriedly remove all the feather and soft down, which was kept for bed pillows. Soft feathers floated everywhere! The week after Christmas might be spent visiting friends and neighbors or exchanging entertaining evening meals. New Years Eve was a special dinner of oyster stew.

My four, older brothers loved to tease me. One winter, one brother talked me into sticking my tongue onto the pump handle of the cistern pump outside the house. Well, it was not easy pulling a tongue off a frozen pump handle! I recall I should have been wise to their tricks on me!

Because the 1930's were dry years, we no longer had the frozen over ponds where ice skating could be enjoyed. Occasionally, there would be some planned entertainment at one of the neighborhood schools. I recall my brothers and Hank Nesseth playing their guitars at one programs. It was great and I miss that music. After refreshments, the crowd would join in games such as London Bridge and Skip To My Lou. Church picnics at Lake Campbell and the fun of inside roller skating was as part of teenage life.

Also, summer socials at homes with lovely yards would furnish an evening of entertainment. At these events, the young folks would sit in the car and watch the old folks visiting and feeding their faces.

There were also Farmer's Union meetings. These were held at night at various homes with much food and lots of visiting. All gathered occasions required lots of coffee, cakes, cookies, and pies. I remember one of those meeting when I was in misery looking at all the good food because I had just had my tonsils out.

Perhaps the most devastating time of the 1930's were the horrible dust storms. I recall one storm in early 1934 when I was searching in some weeds for turkey eggs. Suddenly, I was in such a cloud of dust I could not find my way back to the house. I was scared, but somehow I did get back. I will never forget how the fine dirt sifted onto the window sills in the form of miniature snowbanks.

Another storm occurred when I was staying with my Uncle Arnold and Aunt Signe on the old Rogen farm. Mother had gone to Boone, Iowa to stay with her sister Elma and get some treatments from the doctor there. While I was walking toward the Rogen home from school, I saw a huge cloud of dust rolling towards me from the northwest. I was a quarter mile from the house, and boy, did my legs fly the rest of the way. I just made it to the door when all the flying dust hit.

In the fall of 1935, an arrangement was made for me to attend Brooking High School. My parents paid a weekly rental of a room from Mrs. Olson on Main Street and I cooked private meals on a small kerosene stove which was stuck in an unventilated closet in the room. On Saturday and Sunday, I always spent at home on the farm with church activities on Sunday. This meant much travel for the folks on Friday and Sunday Evenings. Volga High School seemed a lot closer so my second sophomore year commenced there.

However, in November 1936, I returned to the farm and discovered a major decision had been made. The farm and mortgage was being signed over to the older brother Edwin. All our belongings were being sold. Only a precious few treasures and clothing were being packed in a small home-made trailer. Mother and Dad, my younger brother, Marvin, and I were headed to California in a 1936 Chevrolet with a trailer following behind.

I was very disappointed when we moved to California because I received word of an opportunity to join a group to attend The Nations 4-H Club Camp and a trip to Washington, D.C. My team-mate went and compiled a beautiful and detailed description of all their adventures. She sent a copy to me, and I still have this even though it is now a bit yellowed, soiled and tattered.

We stopped a my Mother's sister's home in Boone, Iowa to express our farewells before going to California. I still recall my first glimpse of desert area and the huge Joshua trees. My brother James was in the Navy and located in California. He had arranged for a place for us to stay just east of Torrance, California. His ship would often dock at the Long Beach of San Pedro harbors.

After many disappointments in locating satisfactory employment, my brother Marvin returned to South Dakota. California did not prove to be all that excitable and soon the many changes - the dripping dampness of the Quonset Hut housing, the pungent small of eucalyptus, having to wear a uniform dress at school, and chances for making new friends all became a real drag.

However, time has a way of healing and bringing on new growth. In 1939, I graduated from Torrance High School with 77 other students. Being a commercial major and having experienced a variety of jobs during my school years prepared me for the clerical field. Going on to college had never become even a dream as I had been informed I was very fortunate to receive a high school education.

With a little help from distant relatives, I secured a job with Hartford Insurance located in the heart of Los Angeles. Salaries were small, but a lot could be done with them to help cover costs at home plus personal clothing and some furniture.

My church activities brought new outlets and new friends. I became actively involved in the Luther League and met friends from Anaheim, Compton, Santa Ana, and Long Beach with my responsibilities."

- FBH - South Dakota

•   •   •

THE NORTH

"I was only 4 years old when the crash of October 29, 1929 happened. I was very young, but there are many things that stick out in my mind.

My parents owned and lived on a 900 acre farm in South New Jersey. When the crash came they lost the farm and we had to move to a city. I remember my mother crying as we left the farm in a Model-T Ford with rumble seat and all. We pulled a hand-made trailer with a few of our belongings. It was a very sad trip and it felt as if we were on the road forever.

We moved the Elizabeth, New Jersey where my father went to school to become a barber and my mother cleaned houses for the people who had the money. There were many times when she took me with her and I helped her clean the houses. She was paid $1.00 per day.

We were poor, but we did not know it as mother gave us plenty of love and we ate well. The food may not be what people are used to today, but the meals were always tasty and good.

Christmas was always a happy time and we each got one present. It was always something to wear and we never received toys due to lack of money.

In 1937, my mother, who was a gambling woman, played the Numbers and won $10,000. She invested this money into a car dealership and also Esso (now Exxon) gas stations. My mother put my father and brothers into business. By the time World War II came along, the family was on easy street because of Mom. She was the backbone of our family.

We each had two pairs of shoes. One pair was for weekdays and the other pair was for Sunday. When the ones we wore during the week needed new soles, we used cardboard or newspapers to patch up the hole. After a while, the Sunday shoes were used for the weekdays, and we got new Sunday shoes.

We never really celebrated any birthdays or other holidays with fanfare. We were a close-knit family and love always took the place of worldly things.

We never went hungry, but there were families that were on Home Relief, and it was such a stigma on them; almost like shame. There also were the WPA works that President Roosevelt put to work and these men worked on the roads pulling up rails from trolley cars and then paved the roads."

- New Jersey

·　　　·　　　·

"My mother and I lived with my grandfather during the depression. We never knew there was a depression going on. My grandfather was from the old school and the women in his family did not work no matter how bad the circumstances were.

111

Grandfather worked as a dock worker and never was without a job. He would bring home all kinds of exotic things from the wharves, like bananas and fruits.

The only time I knew that money might be a little bit tight was when my grandfather would slip newspaper in the bottom of his shoes when a hole was worn in them."

- Massachusetts

. . .

"My most vivid memory of the Depression was of people selling apples on the streets and keeping warm around fires.

My saddest moment was the death of my father, but my happiest moment was meeting my future husband and our engagement during these times. I introduced my family to him on Thanksgiving and it remains my favorite holiday.

Gifts consisted of things we needed such as clothing, and clothes were of a minimum supply.

I was a teenager during the Depression and my father was a physician. He lost everything of financial worth in the crash and worried constantly about paying bills. We were not in dire circumstances as so many others were and we were able to maintain a simple lifestyle. My father had plenty of work, but often was not paid."

- New York

. . .

"My mother died when I was very young. I was the youngest of three girls. My father could not cope with us and put us in a Catholic boarding school for girls. We had to wear uniforms and the nuns were very harsh and strict.

The nuns would punish us by rapping our fingers or giving us a switching if we failed to eat all of our food. One of the things they served was creamed chipped beef on toast. To this day, I despise this dish. My older sister would often eat my food and her food so that I would not be punished by the nuns.

We stayed at this school for three years and then our father came to get us. I was terrified of my father. He was a big, burly man who played around a lot. I remember that I used to put rubber bands around the ends of my shoes so that the soles would not flap. I was scared to walk much with my father around. If my shoes flapped in his presence, he got very angry with me."

- Pennsylvania

．　　　．　　　．

"I was born in 1923, so I was seven to 17 years old during the 1930's. I lived all that time with my mother, father, and younger brother in a residential suburb of Pittsburgh, Pennsylvania.

Nothing much happened to our family during that time that makes me remember it as The Great Depression. We had modest means and did not lack adequate food, clothing or simple pleasures. We never had to sell the house, the car, or any possession to make ends meet. We lived frugally, but so did most people we knew. We did not think that was anything unusual.

Therefore, I do not have anything spectacular to report, but I do have a few isolated stories that may be of some value.

During the early 1930's, my father worked as a machinist in a steel mill in Duquesne, Pennsylvania which was another suburb of Pittsburgh. I suspect that pay was not good, and the steel mills often shut down for long periods for lack of business. My father told of how for the big layoffs, the big bosses walked down the floor where all the men were standing at their machines and pointed to who was to be laid off and who was not. This was done when they (the bosses) knew nothing about any of the men and the machines.

My father's parents lived in Duquesne and my grandmother never complained about the soot and dirt that the steel mills put out. She said that dirt meant work, meaning that if the mills were running, it meant dirt, but it also meant jobs. So, she willingly accepted the dirt.

To supplement his income, my father played saxophone and sang tenor in a small dance band that played in nightclubs around Pittsburgh. He drove up to 50 miles away to meet these engagements. As a result, he knew all the back roads and lots of evenings he did not get home until long after my brother and I had gone to bed.

My other grandparents (my mother's mother and father) lived on a farm of about 150 acres. It was about 50 miles east of Pittsburgh near Greens burg on the Conemaugh River. It was hard work for them, but they made a living at it and always had a little left over at the end of the year.

The railroad ran through their farm, with a stop in the nearby village of Livermore. Hoboes (men traveling and looking for work) often got off of freight cars and came to the farm asking for a few days work. My grandfather usually obliged them and had them cut trees in the woods on the farm for posts. He sold these posts to local coal mines for ceiling support posts. My grandmother fed the hoboes and they slept in the barn.

We had relatives in Toronto, Ontario. I remember visiting them a few times with my parents and grandparents. Once they had only stewed tomatoes for supper because that was all they had. I must have been about ten then. My brother and I asked, "Is this all we get?" The parents of the other family were embarrassed. So were my mother and father and they scolded us for saying that. We did not understand, and it had not been explained to us.

My mother's sister married into a wealthy family. They had a country house near Fallingwater, the well-known house that Frank Lloyd Wright designed and built for my uncle's brothers. Our family (my mother, father, brother and I) often went there for vacations with my mother's sister and her family.

A wagon road led from the vacation houses about half a mile down to the Conemaugh River, along which a main-line railroad ran, also. Once several of us walked down to the railroad. Our group included a cousin from the wealthy side of the family who must have been about eight years old. At the side of the railroad, a hobo was cooking something in a large tin can over a small open fire. My young cousin said in astonishment, "He hasn't got a cook!" I suppose that says a lot more about my cousin and his family than it does about the Depression.

I remember my parents saying they would not buy me a Boy Scout uniform when I joined a Boy Scout troop at age twelve. They said we could not afford it. That meant a great deal to me, and I cried, which was rare for me at that age. Because of my reaction, mother and dad relented, and I got my Scout uniform.

I had a small paper route in 1935. I had 20 subscribers and I was age twelve then. We got one cent per day for delivering each paper. The normal route had 30 or 40 subscribers. One boy who was two years older than me had over 50 subscribers. This was really too many, but he explained to me that his father was not working. His newspaper route was the only income for the family. That incident made more of an impression on me than anything else about the effect of the Depression on families. Here was a family subsisting on 50 cents a day, with a 14-year old boy, who was a man before his time, being the breadwinner for the family.

A friend of mine, John Sanks, told me of one episode of his father's experience with the Depression. His father ran a small blueprint duplicating shop. He had one man as a helper. During the depths of the Depression, they scarcely had any customers. If somebody came in to have a copy made (which cost 25 cents), they would use the money to buy lunch. Otherwise, they did not have lunch.

I remember our family going on a traveling vacation about 1933. (We often did that, but it was not an extravagance, because we camped in tents.) We passed through Washington, D.C. during the time World War I veterans were protesting for their pensions that had been promised but never delivered. The veterans had descended on Washington from all over the country.

In downtown parks, we saw the shacks they had built of scrap wood and sheet metal roofing. The men were cooking and warming themselves over open fires made with scrap lumber. I believe the demonstrations were peaceful, and the encampments dissolved after the veterans were promised something toward their pensions. In my mind, this was part of the Depression.

My wife, Martha, does not remember much about the Depression. She lived with her family in a village with no more than a handful of houses in rural South Carolina. They were poor, but not destitute, as were all of her neighbors. Her father always had a regular job. She does not remember her childhood as being anything unusual. She feels that probably most people who lived in the country were better off in hard times than those who lived in cities because they were more self-sufficient.

One other thing about my boyhood experiences also comes to mind. As a boy in the early 1930's, I played with friends in unoccupied houses in the neighborhood. These were well-built, big houses which were left empty, open, and undisturbed. It was spooky, and we were sure there was somebody else there, but of course, there wasn't. The houses evidently were abandoned by their owners because they could not afford to keep them up or make the mortgage payments and there was nobody else who could afford to buy them."

- RH - Pennsylvania

.   .   .

"My father was a Congressman during the Depression. He was very open-hearted to everyone he came into contact with. When people came to him in need, he could not turn them away. His generosity to others almost did the family in.

He said of the Depression, "People went to bed one night as millionaires and woke up the next morning in the gutters waiting for the banks to open that would not unlock their doors."

- Washington, D.C.

.   .   .

"In 1930, I was a freshman in high school. Our town of Needham, Massachusetts was growing rapidly at that time and we were the first class to attend the new beautiful brick school up on the hill. This school is still being used as a high school today.

Our town was a Boston suburb and almost everyone was middle class. There were several estates, but we had no connection with those people. There was also a Polish settlement although most of those families were poor. There was never any prejudice against them or anyone. Everyone was equal.

I do not recall any crime during this time except for the local bank being robbed.

We moved into a new house in 1925. It was one mile on the outskirts from the town. We always walked to school and walked home for lunch and then back again. I estimate we walked four miles each day and feel that may be why I am in general good health now at the age of 79.

I remember Christmas as a happy time. My mother had $100 to buy all the decorations and presents for four children. We all had one main gift and several smaller ones. A lot was made of the stockings. We would drive to Boston to bring two elderly aunts for Christmas and Thanksgiving dinner. They always gave us little boxes or hankies (which we thought was strange).

My father had started a small business with another man and they struggled to keep it going during the Depression. His partner died and after that he really struggled. However, in 1932, he had tried a court case and received $6,000. It was a great day and the company was always successful after that. They paid off the whole mortgage and had money left over. As a result, I never felt the Depression, but many of my friends had a hard time.

I had an older sister so I always had to wear hand-me-downs and I was unhappy about that. My mother always refitted so that I did not look like a rag-a-muffin, but I felt sorely discriminated against.

Probably 20 percent of our class went on to college, but I got a job in Boston with John Hancock Insurance Company. I bought my first car, a Ford Model A, in 1936.

Six girls in my "gang" are still living. We all feel we had a good time to be raised in even if those years were called the Depression years."

- Massachusetts

•   •   •

"I was born in 1922 and was a child during the Depression years. When you are young, you do not worry about everyday things such as paying for groceries, housing, and basic needs. You do not think of tomorrow and enjoy the moment you are experiencing then.

I grew up in New Bronx, New York. I was one of eight children.

People suffered more in the big cities than those who lived on farms because they had to buy everything that was needed. Food was a real big expense. We had a small back yard but it only had room for a few flowers.

My father died in 1933. There was no insurance money or social security to help our family out. Instead, my brother, at age 18, went to work and supported the family. He worked as a tool and die maker making doctor and dentist tools.

My older sister also quit school at age 16. She helped the family by sewing. She made hand-made lingerie.

When I was older, I earned my own money by baby-sitting. The money I earned was my own to keep, and I used it to buy my personal little doodads and knickknacks.

My memory of FDR was good. He did many wonderful things through the CCC, WPA, and other projects for people. He was a very effective president during the Depression years."

- CJ - New York

.   .   .

"In 1930, I was five years old. We had just moved from Jacksonville, Florida to Staten Island, New York. Our move was to allow my father to commute to New York City to his new job. This job was as a draughts man for the Texaco Company, with offices in the recently completed Chrysler building.

My father's salary was minimal. It was just barely enough to pay the rent, put simple food on the table, and buy clothes for our family of four plus his mother who lived with us at the time.

Our clothes were ordered through the Sears catalog and only on an "as needed" basis of once a year. Otherwise, my mother and grandmother stayed busy with sewing, especially mending, darning socks, and altering clothes for our family.

The bungalow we lived in was a rental that was about ten years old. It was electrified with single bare-bulb lighting. My sister and I played in the cellar where the coal-fired furnace which produced steam heat was located.

We played "Store" with empty food cartons, soup cans, and milk bottles. We pasted together paper chains from grocery bags to decorate the "Store." We entered our play area by the only means - a three-foot by five-foot trap door in the kitchen floor located above the cellar.

Our evening meals were often creamed cod fish and boiled potatoes or fried calves liver and creamed onions. We did have some fresh whole milk, which was not homogenized. The cream at the top was used by the adults for their "Postum" (ersatz coffee) and tea.

Sometimes grandmother made cottage cheese from the curds of sour milk she would accumulate. The cheese was made by straining the milk through a large square of scrap muslin. This she would fashion into a small sack tied with string which she had saved up over time. She then placed the sack in the stream of cold water from the kitchen tap to rinse out the sour whey by squeezing the sack repeatedly with her hands. The yield was small, but good with salt and pepper. We all got a little. My sister, Lucy, seemed not to like it nearly as much as I did!"

- LPW - New York

.   .   .

"The fall of 1929 meant more to me than the crash of the New York stock market. That was the year I met a soft-spoken young college student, who later became my husband.

My aunt met this quiet young man first. She shared a seat on the Pennsylvania Railroad from Newark, New Jersey to Spring Lake, New Jersey. He was going to visit a high school friend. During the course of the trip, she discovered he was a student at New York University. She told him her niece had applied at the same school. One thing led to another, and she invited him to my home for Sunday dinner.

When I first saw him, he did not impress me though he was neatly dressed, of average height, about five-feet nine-inches tall, with a beautiful smile and a lovely, smooth brown complexion. He confessed somewhat later that I did not set him afire either!

However, we finally found a pleasant relationship. Eurie was employed in New York and had Sundays free, so that was when he visited. Since money was not in abundance and we lived a state apart, there were no movie dates or anything in Verona, New Jersey. However, I received an invitation to visit with Eurie's family that consisted of his brother, sister-in-law, and a cousin. Then, in New York City, we saw a Broadway show and a football game.

There were more visits, but the dates were not those which cost a lot of money. So, we made do with walks and rides on the Fifth Avenue bus. One weekend after knowing Eurie for almost two years, he asked me to marry him. We were on the upper deck of a Fifth Avenue bus. The next Sunday I received a ring. It was purchased with great sacrifice and presented proudly. For a college student on his own in New York City, I am sure it meant much penny pinching.

We made plans to be married in my parents' home on a Sunday afternoon in September. The house was decorated lovingly with snapdragons, zinnias, and whatever fall flowers that were in my father's garden. My aunt, the wife of my father's brother, played the piano. I settled on an outfit that could double as a going-away outfit also. Although my parents had jobs, money was not plentiful. However, my Mom made a cake, little sandwiches, and punch. To me, it was a beautiful affair surrounded by family and a couple of girl friends.

Then, we were off on a three-day honeymoon to Atlantic City! In my purse was a brand new five dollar bill given to em through the courtesy of the aunt who had arranged the meeting of her niece and a wonderful, young college student."

- R. McFadden - New Jersey

. . .

"The Great Depression was a tragic time during the 1930's. My parents owned a four-story brick building which housed cold flats. We lived on the first floor at 24 Bright Street in Jersey City, New Jersey.

My Pop was a boatman on a tugboat which pulled floats along the Hudson River. He brought home a weekly salary which Mom apportioned to pay our bills, and the mortgage was first. We were concerned about our neighbors who were hard hit during this time when they had no income.

One day, I observed as we sat on park benches lining our front steps that when Mom called us home at the regular time for supper, Helen, our neighbor, kept on sitting on the bend and did not go into her flat.

'Mom,' I said, after Pop gave the blessing for our food. 'Helen did not go to her home for supper.'

Mom said to our father, 'Joseph, tomorrow our soup will have more water so I can send some over to the Welgos' family.'

Pop only frowned as he knew Mom would do as she pleased. Later that day, she sent me with a loaf of her homemade bread and homemade jam over to my friend, Helen's home.

My Mom always sliced everything thicker or thinner depending on whom we shared our food with because we always shared with those in need. Those were the days I saw men selling apples and even pencils on street corners. I saw what we called 'bread lines' where people in need lined up to get a loaf of bread. It was a time when five cents could buy a loaf of bread, and even a penny went a long way.

I could buy an ice cream cone for three cents at the local stores on Barrow Street, but I had to get Mom's permission because she did not want me to eat an ice cream cone when our neighbors could not afford three cents for one. It was a time when families had many children. On our block alone, I played with about fourteen children on the street. The street was empty as very few people owned a car.

Mrs. Stella Jankoweski, our local mid-wife, won a Ford at a church raffle. She was a local celebrity as she delivered babies day and night, and too often was never paid. We were so happy that our street had one car and would all look at it in wonderment.

Pop, Mom, and us kids always ate together at the supper table. We were not allowed to converse until after we ate the hot food prepared by Mom cooking on the black, wood-burning stove. This stove heated only the kitchen while all the rest of our home was cold.

We wore hand-knitted sweaters that Mom knitted or crocheted. My two sisters and I, after we washed, dried and put away the dishes in the cupboard, often sat with our feet in the open oven door to keep warm when the wood flared up the heat. Mom told us stories of her homeland in Poland and taught us Polish songs.

I remember every Saturday Mom would scrub the kitchen linoleum floor and the lay newspaper upon it to keep it clean. Late Saturday night, she would remove the newspapers in preparation for Sunday. I loved Sundays as no hard physical work was allowed. We would dress in Sunday clothes and go to church. My Mom loved to cook, and upon our return, she would don an apron, freshly starched and ironed, to cover her dress as she made the most delicious chicken soup and homemade noodles she had prepared the day before. She had purchased the freshly killed chicken the day before on Brunswick Street where live chickens were sold.

My sisters and I would read the Sunday New York News while Pop would lay down in the bedroom off of the kitchen. In our home, we led a rather sheltered life depending entirely on our parents who dictated what was expected of us and we obeyed.

We never locked our door except at night after we said our prayers on our knees, and Pop wound the alarm clock. The signals of the Depression years were all about us, but life for us meant Mom, Pop, and our immediate family. We empathized with our neighbors and shared what we had. Mom was always educating our neighbors in way to save, but those times gave our neighbors very little to save as to them daily living was difficult."

- F Moeller - New Jersey

.   .   .

"I am indeed one person who went through many difficult years without faltering. I have just celebrated my One Hundredth birthday. I was born March 22, 1895 in Boston, Massachusetts.

I grew up in comfortable circumstances. I was the youngest of seven children. Our parents were devoted to us, and being the baby of the family, they apparently spoiled me badly. I knew warmth, security, and loads of love. This gave me the background to be able to survive adversity when it struck. This background gave me the courage and strength to help my husband with a serious illness in the 1930's.

The Depression years were difficult for me - extremely so. I had a ill husband and three children, but we managed. Our children lived these years happily and never realized how we struggled to pay the rent! Even though we told them we could not buy them the luxuries in food and clothes that we would like to give them, the children never went hungry and understood our problems.

During the 1930's, my husband became seriously ill. This illness appeared unexpectedly and baffled the doctors. Then, they found the cause.

Back in 1917-1918, a devastating epidemic of influenza swept Europe during World War I. It hit the United States in 1918. Most people died in this epidemic, but my husband caught this flu and survived. Now, in 1931, the doctors found the germs of the flu had settled into one of his kidneys.

After six weeks in the hospital, they operated and removed the kidney. Then, he began to recover - very slowly.

My husband had been manager of a dry cleaning plant. During the Depression, this company was struggling for existence and the owners left us high and dry without any income when my husband became sick.

It was the height of winter now. I used our savings to pay for rent, food, and the coal delivery.

Before the surgery, I went to the surgeon and told him of my financial plight. I promised I would pay his fee gradually because I did not have the money to give all at once. Since I was honest about it, he said he would be glad to work with me.

'However,' he said, 'this is a critical operation. Your husband must have round-the-clock nursing. You must be able to pay the RN's for their services.'

I looked at my dwindled bank balance. I could not discuss my problems with my husband because the poison from the kidney had affected his mind as well.

I determined there was no one to ask except the bank. When I went there, I was politely told we were a good risk in ordinary times, but these were not ordinary times. They could no longer loan money on promises regardless of the good intentions.

Then, I sat down and wrote letters to my brothers. I told them about the circumstances. They both mailed me enough money to tide me over for a few weeks. They were also feeling the pinch of the times, but they knew our situation was critical.

The operation was successful. I paid the nurses and my husband came home to recuperate.

I finally told him I had not received a salary check since his illness. I explained what I had done to handle the situation.

Our children at that time were 6, 11, and 13. They managed well since I spent most of my time at the hospital. I did prepare their meals before I left the house in the morning. The two older children took care of the youngest, who was in first grade. My son, the oldest, became head of the family, and they all got along fine. He came directly home after school and watched the furnace.

During my husband's long months of convalescence, he developed a product called 'Lestoil.' It had great cleaning abilities in laundering, cleaning woodwork, carpets, etc. with never a scratch or other problem. My husband had graduated from Harvard and was a man of vision. The product and he became famous as the first television spot advertiser on the market in the early days of television. So, we became successful.

In our last 40 years, we traveled the world and never forgot to give freely of our bounty to worthwhile charities. We received great satisfaction in doing so.

I wrote a book titled 'The Two of Us' so that our descendants would not forget the great man from whom they are descended.

He and I knew plenty of adversity during the difficult years of the 1930's, but he never allowed his three children to go hungry, showed interest in their schooling and education, and always showed them love."

- AMB - Massachusetts

.   .   .

<u>CONCLUSION</u>

The resiliency of a generation who suffered so much hardship in their youth and early adulthood has been set down by these few stories of the 1930's.

This was a generation who had no television to watch in their youth or computer and video games to play. Instead, they created their own toys and games from simple everyday items.

This generation had real fears when illness came because there was no penicillin. This generation pooled their assets together in order to survive because there were few organized charities to step in and ease the pain. Their cautious, careful, frugal attitudes created by those hungry years of want have added to our nation's wealth because of their experiences.

This book was a great learning experience for me because I am a child of a generation who never have suffered great hardship, but if hardship and trials ever do come my way, I will use these pages as my reference book so that I, too, will persevere, change, and survive.

Following is my last interview. The knowledge and memory of this wonderful person I had the privilege to speak to was vast, and she had things to say not only about the 1930's but also comments on our society of today.

"In 1932, I was 18 years old and had just graduated from high school. Our school was not accredited. Therefore, I had to find a job in order to help my family.

I found one at a cotton mill. I worked from 6 p.m. in the evening until 5 a.m. the next morning. I started out working for $4.85 a week.

I feel the Depression started in 1928. There was a big housing boom in Florida at that time. The expansion went bust, the money supply began to slow down, the stock market crashed, and the banks closed.

I recall many people lost everything they had. There were many suicides committed by jumping from buildings.

My father was a farmer, and my mother was a homemaker. I was next to the youngest in a family of 13 children of which 10 survived into adulthood.

Our farm was rented because my father had lost our family farm a few years before. It was about 200 acres. During the Depression, my father had three men help him on the farm. They were paid $3.00 a week. He also furnished them with a house and land to garden. My father used these men all year long. He did not let them go when the fields were idle. Instead, he put them to work chopping wood.

At 18, girls were considered to be adults. (Boys had to wait until they were 21 to come of age.) Because of this, I cast my first vote and it was for Franklin

D. Roosevelt. I voted for FDR because Hoover was a bad president in my opinion. I felt FDR offered better opportunity for change.

During my senior year in high school, I only had two dresses. One was to wash and one was to wear. Job opportunities for women were very poor. The professions of teaching or secretarial work were considered acceptable jobs for women. I had a hard time finding a job, but eventually did at a cotton mill.

My wages went to help the family. Most of my older brothers and sisters were married with children to raise. We helped them out with items from the farm.

We plowed our fields with mules and grew our own wheat for flour and corn for cornmeal or grits. My mother fixed three meals a day, and for each meal, she made 40 biscuits and a big loaf of cornbread.

In addition to helping my older brothers and sisters, I also used my money to help my younger brother go to business school. I felt it was more important for him to get the extra schooling.

Our meals were nothing elaborate. We had our own eggs, butter, and milk. Mother always had sweets. I remember her tea cakes and sweet potato pie with fondness.

We did not eat lots of beef. Pork could be salted or smoked while beef did not keep because we had no refrigeration.

Our light came from kerosene lamps. Our kitchen was separated by a breezeway from the house. It was built apart for two reasons. The first was because of the potential of fire, and the second because the kitchen was fiercely hot in the summertime. My mother cooked our food on a wood burning stove, and in the winter, we would stay in the kitchen in order to be warm.

During these years, there were no locked doors. There were also no screens to keep the flies and mosquitoes out. We did have thumb latch locks, but anybody could come in. We all looked to our father as the protector, and we all felt we were safe when he was home.

Things were cheap during the Depression. A three-pound can of Maxwell House coffee was 25 cents, five pounds of sugar - 19 cents, one pound of salt bacon - three cents a pound, one pound of steak - 25 cents, unsliced bread - five cents. Shoes were $1.95, underwear - 25 cents, and a dress was $2.00. Five dollars could have bought an entire wardrobe and ten dollars could buy lots of groceries, but during the 1930's, no one had that ten dollars to buy anything with. There was also no credit. If you could afford it, things were put on lay-away for fifty cents a week.

Birthdays were always celebrated with a cake and a small gift. The gift was either home-made or a necessity such as a pair of shoes.

My mother sewed everything. She made our bras and underclothes. She even made my father's suits and shirts. She did not buy yards of fabric. She bought bolts. If we received anything ready-made, we felt we were living high.

My father had only one arm. Because of this, he did not hunt or fish. My father also traded pea seed so that he could get a car for me so that I could get around.

In the 1930's, FDR began projects like the CCC and WPA. In order to get aid, you had to work. The government also began to furnish commodities of beans, meat, and food to people.

FDR also cut my work day to eight hours a day, 40 hours a week. I also saw my pay increase to $12.50 a week.

FDR also began social security. However, this was no help for my father because he was a farmer, and at that time, farmers were considered self-employed.

My memories of the 1930's were that people were happy and everybody was in the same boat. My parents taught us in early childhood that work never hurt anybody. They gave us good examples by working right beside us in the fields. The 1930's also made families stay close together. Because we stuck together and helped each other out, it created a strong bond with all of us that we carried all through our lives.

I sincerely believe everybody should experience what we did during the Depression. It taught us how to save and share, and what mattered the most in our lives which were our church and our families."

- EB - South Carolina

.   .   .

ABOUT THE AUTHOR

Published in national and local publications, Ms. Anderson salutes a unique generation with this book.